In the Silence of My Heart

Volumes 8,9,10

Kathleen McCarthy

CONTENTS

Volume 8:   All Prophecies in the Year 2015
Volume 9:   All Prophecies in the Year 2016
Volume 10:   All Prophecies in the Year 2017

DECLARATION

Since the abolition of Canon 1399 and 2318 of the former Code of Canon Law by Paul VI in AAS58 (1966), publications about new apparitions, revelation, prophecies, miracles, etc. have been allowed to be distributed and read by the Faithful without the express permission of the Roman Catholic Church providing that they contain nothing which contravenes faith and morals. This means no Imprimatur is necessary. The Author wishes to manifest unconditional submission to the final and official judgment of the Magisterium of the Roman Catholic Church regarding the material contained herein.

A Nihil Obstat and Imprimatur attest that the work itself has not been found harmful to the faith and morals of the faithful. They are not endorsements of any claims of private revelations, apparitions, visions, prophecies, or miracles that may be found in the work.

FORWARD

We read in the Book of Ezekiel (Chapter 37:4-10):

"Then he said to me: Prophesy over these bones and say to them: Dry bones hear the word of the LORD! Thus says the Lord GOD to these bones: Listen! I will make breath enter you so you may come to life. I will put sinews on you, make flesh grow over you, cover you with skin, and put breath into you so you may come to life. Then you shall know that I am the LORD. I prophesied as I had been commanded. A sound started up as I was prophesying rattling like thunder. The bones came together, bone joining to bone. As I watched, sinews appeared on them, flesh grew over them, skin covered them on top, but there was no breath in them. Then he said to me: Prophesy to the breath, prophesy son of man and say to the breath: Thus says the Lord GOD: From the four winds come O breath and breathe into these slain that they may come to life. I prophesied as he commanded me and the breath entered them; they came to life and stood on their feet, a vast army."

How should the reader approach the messages contained in this book? If you approach it merely as a devotional that you read to gain strength for your day, you will surely be inspired but you will not get the full benefit this book has to offer you.

If you approach this with a sense of awe of how the Holy Spirit works through Kathleen McCarthy, you will receive a great example for your own relationship with the Holy Spirit but you will not get the full benefit this book has to offer you.

If you use these messages to be guided on doing the will of God the Father you will be closer to *"Thy will be done on Earth as it is in Heaven"*, but you will not get the full benefit this book has to offer you.

What must you do to get the full benefit this book has to offer you? Approach this book like dry bones eager to be animated by God's very life for these words have the power of prophesy! The power of prophesy is more than inspiration, instruction, or correction, though it is all of these things. The power of prophecy is animation! Becoming animated by God's life, truth and love.

Approaching this book as dry bones disposes us in humility to acknowledge our total dependency on God and that he is the source of our very life. Anything that we accomplish for Him must be animated by Him. This book is for everyone who is seeking to be animated by God whether you are a teen, a stay at home mom, a priest, a business owner, in a nursing home, etc. The messages in this book will help you to be animated by God Himself in whatever circumstances come your way.

Fr. Stephen P. DeLacy

INTRODUCTION

About Ten years ago, Thirty years after my own conversion, I was sitting in Adoration, where I felt The Lord speak to my heart saying: "Place My broken body in the arms of My Mother, there, The Holy Spirit will fill them with new life. I want one mystical body in My body." And so I did, ever since I have prayed for unity in the universal church. I have prayed that all would become one. One Holy, Catholic and Apostolic Church.

About Two years ago at prayer during Adoration, I was prompted by The Holy Spirit to deliver a message. A message with an urgency to "Ready My people", to speak about our Baptismal call and the new life of the Spirit of God within each baptized Christian which enables and empowers us to be authentic witnesses. Although I spoke about these things many times in the past Forty years of my apostolate, there was as I stated a sense of urgency, a new anointing to deliver this message. I was instructed to take this message wherever The Lord sent me to speak throughout the Church. I was told as I did so, many hearts would be set on fire and minds would be enlightened to the Truth and Sacramental Life of our one Holy, Catholic and Apostolic Church. Souls would come back to the Church through grace as The Word of The Lord was spoken. Many would be healed and delivered from darkness by Sacramental Grace and be infused with power to go and make disciples. "This is a time of a tremendous outpouring of The Holy Spirit on the Church and her faithful priests. A time of mercy and grace, flowing from My heart, through My priests to My people."

In July of 2009 while being at an Eileen George Retreat, Three individuals told Dennis Nolen to look me up and so he called me. After a brief conversation, relating to me how he was directed to me, he said he would come to the Corpus Christi Prayer Group in Upper Gwynedd, PA the next Thursday evening. After a month or so, Dennis asked me if he could record my prophecies. I said "No, this is where people share from their hearts." He continued, stating that of course he realized that and only wanted to record the messages I spoke and then would print them out for the group and distribute them each Thursday, as he felt they were meant for everyone to read and think about. Again, I said "No". Just that quickly, The Lord spoke to my heart and said only, "Yes". I immediately told Dennis, "You may record them". With puzzlement, he said but you just said "No?" Smiling I said, but The Lord just said "Yes."

So it began, Dennis started to record the prophetic utterances I believe The Lord was speaking in and through me. It will suffice only to say some began to share these words with others and many other lives were impacted and much fruit of The Spirit was being manifested in their lives including Dennis Nolen's own life.

Dennis and his lovely wife, Anne and beautiful daughter, Alex and I have become good friends, for this too I praise God.

Over Twenty-five years ago, when I finally responded to The Lord's call on me to begin to write, I received the words: "In the Silence of My Heart" as a title. I even had an artist draw it as I saw it in my mind's eye. When I wrote my first book, I was ever so surprised when I was led to title it: "What the World needs now."

I asked The Lord, what about "In the Silence of My Heart?" The response I received was, "You will know when and how to use it."

My Second book which I am in the midst of writing is to be called: "He is Alive", a book about Jesus' Eucharistic Presence in my own life.

When would I ever use "In the Silence of My Heart" I wondered?

Well, shortly after these particular prophecies began to be recorded, I knew with absolute certainty, the words were coming from within, "In the Silence of My Heart" as I listened to God's whispers.

Hence, as the recordings are compiled into one volume, I now know this is the time to use this title: "In the Silence of My Heart."

On December 19, 2009, I was led to call Dennis, telling him the first prophecy of September 10, 2009 to the last one of Advent, December 17, 2009, was to be signed "Volume I" and be put aside for now. I said I didn't know why, but had a sense there may be a "Volume II" and I would wait on The Lord for direction.

Kathleen McCarthy

Volume 8

Nihil Obstat
Rev. Msgr. Joseph G. Prior

Imprimatur
Archbishop Charles J. Chaput
Archiepiscopus Philadelphiensis
October 18, 2018

No portion of this book may be reproduced in any form without written permission from the Publisher:
Morning Star – New Dawn Ministries
P.O. Box 1446
Blue Bell, PA 19422
If unavailable in local bookstores, additional copies of this book may be purchased by writing to the Publisher at the above address.

Copyright, 2019 By Kathleen McCarthy
ALL RIGHTS RESERVED   ISBN 978-0-9641873-4-4

Artwork by Margaret M. Matt

PROPHECIES

1/8/15

I am the Alpha and the Omega ... the first and the last, the beginning and the end. I tell you in a very special way that I am close to the brokenhearted. I want to bind up their wounds, I want to heal their hearts and I want to comfort their soul. The ways of the world will draw you away from me. It will entice you, lure you, speak of things that will give you fleeting moments of joy, fleeting moments of feeling good inside, and yet they do not last. You see, apart from me there is no good that will last.

This word I give you this night is to comfort your heart and heal your soul. I see every tear that you have ever shed. I have seen you when you've fallen and I've seen you when you've gotten up again and turned to me for grace and help and strength. You have been the recipient of my love before you were even in your mother's womb and throughout your life.

The greatest discipleship is to love me with all your mind and all your heart, all your soul and all your strength. For you see, it is then that I will work within you and through you. I will bring back the lost sheep. I will heal and restore minds, bodies, spirits. I have created you. I have formed and fashioned you with my own hands. Before you were born I knew you. I love you. There's things that you do not understand because my ways are not your ways. I know you often think you have all the answers and you know God wouldn't do "this" and He wouldn't do "that". Do you know the mind of God? I hear it said time and time again, and I, I who show you through all the signs and wonders, through my presence … through the supreme gift, the very source and summit of my presence in this world, in the Eucharist … my own body, my own blood, my own mind, my own Spirit given for you, given to you that you might come to know that "I AM", that you might come to believe that I am Lord over every single situation in your life: illness, sickness, debt, brokenness, woundedness, emotional illness, physical illness, spiritual illness. I am the Lord your God. Do you think that I am not Lord over every situation? I am all power. I am all love. I am all mercy. This is the discipleship I want you to know. I want you to follow my example. I want you to be that "Christ-giver". I want you to be the one that reaches out in mercy, love, forgiveness.

There are many who are broken and wounded and hurting. There are many who are suffering financially. There are many who have hopes and dreams and I will use many of you to be a part of those hopes, those dreams, that they might see my hand, that they might see me in the midst of their suffering, in the midst of their doubts, in the midst of their fears. So I would have you share this truth with others. I would have you be my disciple, my students, to go out into the world and make new disciples. There is a world in waiting of truth and love and hope and mercy … many of those in your own families.

Will you take this message? Will you deliver it, not only in word, but especially in action? So go therefore. If you love me with all your mind, all your heart, all your soul and all your strength, then you watch and be in awe of the miracle of my love and my power in your life and in the lives of those you bring the good news to. So go therefore. Be filled with my power, my light, my love and ignite a fire in the hearts of all those who are in need of the warmth of my love.

1/15/15

I call each and every one of you by name. By name I have called each of you. I have a work and a plan for each and every person. You wonder what you can do … one person? You can do your best and trust me to do everything else in you and through you to accomplish the work that I've called you to do. A general would not march into battle without strategically planning every step of the journey. Many of you have gone on trips and traveled. I've taken you many places. Would you think of traveling without first checking the climate, without first looking into where you'll be staying and preparing your trip before you even leave? No, of course not. You pack your clothes according to the weather conditions. You take everything that you need to accomplish everything that you are called to do on that trip whether it's for pleasure or business. You see, each of you are on a journey. You're traveling the road to eternal life, and there are many road blocks. There are many twists and turns on the journey. There are many detours along the way, and there are many temptations and distractions to try to confuse you and take you off the road that I have set you upon, and given you the tools and the necessary gifts of the Spirit that will safeguard your trip.

And so it is with the spiritual journey. I have given much to my Church. I alone have instituted my one, holy, catholic and apostolic Church, and within this Church I have given you the safeguards so that you would not collapse on the way to your eternal destiny. I have given you grace, healing, strength, love and mercy for the journey. As you eat my body and drink my blood you receive my life within you. You see, it'll be my strength working in you and through you when you avail yourself to the sacrament of love and mercy itself ... my Eucharistic Presence. Your tender and loving God, in every tabernacle all over the world, waits to feed you and to nourish you and to strengthen you. I leave you the sacrament of reconciliation and healing so that when you fall you would turn to me and I will raise you up. I will heal your heart. I will ease your burden. I will stretch out my hand and send my word forth and wash away your sins through my infinite love and mercy. Never think your sin or a sin of another is greater than my mercy. Never allow yourself to be that self-absorbed to think that you and the sins that you have fallen into are greater than my mercy. Did I not lay down my life and go to the cross for each and everyone? I died for all that all might have life to the full.

So on this spiritual journey as you travel in the world to your eternal reward, know that I go before you and prepare the way. I send guardian angels, your own guardian angel, to do my bidding in your life. I whisper in the silence of your heart to go this way or that way. I send you to those who can guide you and lead you on the path that you're supposed to go forward on … the path to grow and develop into what I call you to be.

So use those gifts. Calculate, estimate, make a strategic plan in your life that nothing, no one, or no thing will draw you off the path to eternal life. Make frequent use of the sacraments. Come together to praise and thank me. Sing songs of worship. Keep your eyes and your heart and your mind and your spirit set on me, for I solemnly assure you this: no one will snatch out of my hand what I have claimed to bring home to my Father. It is only you, you with your free choice, you with your free will … it is only you. The decisions are yours day in and day out. And when you turn to me for grace, I will bless you from your head to your toes. my forgiveness will bring health and healing to your mind, body, and spirit.

I did count the cost and I paid it in full for each and every one of you that you might be where I am.

1/22/15

My people continue to seek answers from all the wrong places. They seek to find answers for all the questions that they have in their mind and in their heart, and yet they have not come to the fullness of truth that I alone, I myself, am all wisdom, all knowledge, all light, all truth, all goodness. I seek to infuse my wisdom, my knowledge into each of you and to all those who listen to hear my voice and to seek my will.

I asked you before: Do you think you know the mind of God? I alone reveal to my people the fullness of truth, the light indeed that dispels the darkness of confusion and doubt and misunderstanding. Man runs after the wisdom of the world and time and time again mankind becomes more and more confused. Time and time again they seek deeper thrills, more pleasure, more power, but nothing is lasting. I alone am the way, the truth and the life. You see, I enlighten minds. I infuse every being with gifts of wisdom and knowledge and understanding. I give them gifts of intellect. I give them gifts of love and mercy and compassion, but they pick and choose the gifts they want.

But it is to you, it is to you that I speak. It is to you that I reveal day in and day out the mysteries of faith, the mysteries of love. I am love and I seek to love every single person. I seek to love them into wholeness where they are broken and wounded. The more they let go and allow me to move in them and through them they will be blessed, they will be free, they will be able to grow into all that I call them to be. Many ask where I'm at all the time. Where is God in the midst of this? I'm in their midst, but they look within themselves for the answers or they look to the world, and they want it fixed instantly. This is not my way. My way is to teach you. My way is to reveal truth to you, to form you and fashion you, to enlighten your mind and understanding a little bit more the more you surrender to me. The more you surrender, the more power, the more love, the more wisdom and knowledge and grace I will pour into you. So you seek, you see, the mind of God. You seek my wisdom. You ask for my intervention and then you will see. Your eyes will be opened and your minds will understand that I am already at work. I am already in the midst of working through your situations and circumstances. I am in the midst of healing you emotionally, giving you stability as you've never had before, giving you glimpses of the magnificent gift of my love unconditionally shed on the cross for everyone. You are beginning to understand this truth.

You seek my wisdom. You want to walk in my way and you want to follow the path that I have laid before you, and tonight I say to you I am well pleased. I am well pleased that you seek my way and not the world's way. I am pleased that when you fail you get right up again and turn to me for grace, guidance and direction. For the world will fail you time and time again but I will never fail you. The choice is yours, not mine. I give you my love and all that I have I give to you a little bit more every day when you surrender to my way over your way. Take this message into your heart and I will bless it and anoint that word, my living word, at work in your heart transforming your lives, conforming your life, as truly children of the most high God.

1/29/15

I call you to listen. I call you to listen with the ear of your heart, for I dwell deep within your heart and your soul. I tell you that I want you to begin to take some quiet time so that you can not only listen but that you can hear my word with your heart, with your mind, and your understanding. I want you to listen for I will guide you myself and lead you. I would not have you worry about the future. I would not have you stuck in the past. I want you to be with me in the present. I want you to go to my word and remember and imagine me walking with you, talking with you, just as I did when I walked upon the earth for I still walk with you now you know. I want to converse with you. I want to speak in the silence of your heart. I want to take you from glory to glory. I have brought you here so that you might grow more fully into what I'm calling you to be. I want you to remember that if you keep your eyes and your heart and mind set on me and not on the problems at hand, I will bring peace where there's turmoil.

      I ask you to come a little closer to my mother. For you see, just as I was given to the world through her … I took my flesh from her … I look like her … and so much of my life on earth was because of how she taught me to listen to my Father … the Father's desire now in this time is that you would listen to me. I want you to experience my mercy, the tenderness of my heart, but at the same time the power, the magnitude of the love that I have for you. You will never grasp it fully or completely. But from glory to glory I will fashion you and mold you and transform you by the renewal of your mind. It'll not be from a book. It'll be from my heart to your heart. I will teach you, guide you, lead you. I will heal you and strengthen you so that when others come to you they will know that I am the God of the living and not of the dead because they will see me in you. They will begin to understand that I have come to reveal myself more fully, personally to each one. I have called you to be here. For a time such as this you were born, and I will fashion and mold you and transform you and conform you more perfectly to my likeness and image as you continue to surrender into my heart. Surrender your life into my hands and know that apart from me you will not be able to bear any fruit that will last.

So I call you to listen. Listen to those that I've placed in your life. Listen to my Holy word that is proclaimed in the readings at Mass. Listen to my anointed ones preach. You see, my word is living and effective. It is in listening with the ear of Your heart, it is in surrendering your life into my hands, it is in being a contradiction to the world that you will be able to lead others to me. I have a plan. I have a plan for not only your life but I have a plan for every single life that I created.

Will you listen? Will you have ears that hear and eyes that see, or will you go running after the things that you want of this world? Do not let any person, place or thing have power over you that would rob you of peace, of grace, of strength and joy. I said come and follow me, not go out into the world and follow the ways of the world. So come and follow me.

2/12/15

I love it when you come to me, when you offer me praise, when you come to me in thanksgiving, when you come to me in sorrow, when you come when you're confused and when you doubt. I know as I hear all of your problems, all of your burdens … *"Ah, Ha"*, they finally get it. They turn to me that I might bring joy in the deepest of their sorrows. They turn to me for peace when there's so much turmoil that they are dealing with, and, yes, when lonely I bring consolation, I bring my presence. And in brokenness you turn to me because you know the truth that it is I alone who can put all the pieces together and make you whole. For some it took a long time to come to the realization that they are my sons and daughters, flesh of my flesh and bone of my bone, and that I wait, I wait until they turn to me. And again I say *"Ah, Ha"*, they understand.

There is nothing too difficult to give me. There is no sin so great that my love and mercy can not forgive. Your anxiety and your fears, your questions … I am here to minister to every aspect of your life. Yes, it is humbling. You indeed humble yourself and turn to me because you recognize your own weakness. You can not change your situations or your circumstances and you are often at a loss to know which way to go when you have a decision to make, but yet, you turn to me. You cry out to me. You come to me with expectant faith and again *"Ah, Ha"*, they understand I am the solution, the remedy, the answer, and then I build up trust in your heart, in your mind and in your spirit to know that I and I alone can make all things new. When you surrender to me and let go of the things that you think are the best things for you, when you surrender them to me, I will fill that void in ways that you can not even possibly understand while you're still holding on to what you want, to what you think is best for you. All the manipulation will not change your circumstance. You see I am in the midst, truly in the midst, of every moment, every second, of these situations and circumstances. One day you will look back and you will say, *"Thank you Jesus, my Lord and my God, that you did not answer my prayers in the way I asked"*, for I know all things and I work it all together for a greater good. I am not here to make you happy. I am here that you would become holy.

I speak to your heart this night and ask you to hold this truth in your heart so when you falter, when you doubt, when you're dismayed, when you feel like giving up, this word will well up within you and dispel all that negativity and fill you with a confident assurance that I am indeed not only with you but working in you and through you for my good pleasure. Do not let the world, your pride, keep you from my grace. Continue to come to me and I will fill you with every blessing.

2/19/15

I would have you remember that my joy is your strength. It's a joy that comes from me, you see. I want you to have joy, my joy, that will be complete in you. my joy is indeed your strength. I tell you this because these are tumultuous times and what is needed in these times is a steady faith and trust and hope in me in these times of darkness, confusion ... in these times of hatred and anger that are manifested in so many ways in the world today, beginning sometimes in your own families, in your parishes, in your neighborhoods, in the workplace, on the TVs, on the radio. Many times you hear of the things that would frighten or incapacitate some. These are the times that I pour forth my grace. These are the times that I pour out my Spirit upon you that you might walk in the light in the midst of darkness. You see it is your light, my light that shines through you, that you will bring into the world.

      I alone am the hope. I alone will safeguard your mind and your heart and your spirit if you surrender yourself to me. Surrender your fears and your anxieties ... surrender to me so that again I might fill you with my strength. My joy gives you strength because my joy is the joy of the Father and the Son and the Holy Spirit ... Triune God. It is our strength that will be your strength when you look to me when you are sad, anxious, afraid, confused. There will be much that will try to rob you of peace and incapacitate you from doing the work for which I call you to do, to take my mercy out into the world, to be a light shining brightly to dispel the darkness, to be a voice speaking out with courage and holy boldness. The weak, the broken, the hurt, the physically and emotionally and spiritually challenged ... they are in desperate need now of those who I send into the world to bring them peace, comfort, consolation, strength. Remember my words, that they would know you are Christians by my love, not your love, because in the face of tragedy and turmoil and upheaval your love will not withstand the trial, but my love working in you and through you will give you a peace when so many have lost peace, will give you hope when so many have no hope, will give you boldness and courage for those who shrivel up with fear.

I am an all-powerful God and I am a God who shares His power with His people. There is only one true God in three divine persons. I am the God who created you, I am the God that saved you, and I am the God who empowers you to be everything that I call you to be so that you will lack nothing.

This indeed is an hour of great mercy, not a time to be afraid or woe, but a time to take this mercy out to all those who are in need of mercy and they do not realize it. You see, you know you need mercy. You know you need a peace that goes beyond your own understanding. You know that you need a love that loves even unconditionally, but there are so many who do not understand that love.

I am always present. I am the eternal word and the eternal Now. So when you place your hope and trust in me, you will not be ashamed but you will rejoice for I will watch over you and protect you and guide you and lead you. I ask you to open your hearts so that I might fill your heart with great courage. Open your mind so that I can reveal things to you beyond your understanding. Open your eyes that I might give you vision. A people without vision perish and so I give you my vision. Be watchmen and watchwomen and let your light shine brightly in the darkness, for I have overcome the darkness.

2/26/15   (1 of 2)

Do not wait until tomorrow for the things that you want to do to make yourself right … right with others, right with me. You see, I only promise you "today". My love is eternal and forever. My promises are true, but you have only been promised "now", and so I tell you that I love you and I want you to come to me. I don't want you to wait until you feel you're in perfect shape to come to me. You see, all my people are out of shape, but it is in coming to me that I will reform, transform you with my word, with the fire of my love and with the power of my Spirit. Do not wait. When you have a word, speak it. When you can mend a quarrel, do it; do not wait till tomorrow. You know not what tomorrow will bring.

2/26/15   (2 of 2)

So many today, so many just compromise their faith, compromise their beautiful catholic faith. It will get harder and harder to stand firm because many will walk away, many will deny my presence, many will deny their faith, many will deny their religion out of fear. It's the greatest tactic that the evil one uses time and time again. He likes to strike fear in the hearts of my people. He likes to lie to you, deceive you. He deprives you of peace and joy and strength and hope because you believe what you see going on around you and fear strikes in your heart. This is all an illusion, you need not fear anything. I am your reality. I alone am the truth. I give you my way to walk in and I call you to follow the way that I provide you to walk in.

I teach you through my holy word. I've left you mother Church to guide you and lead you and strengthen you in the sacraments. I come to you in Holy Communion so that I may truly rest in you, fill you, fill the empty places, heal the broken hearts. Where there is darkness in your heart, in your mind or in your spirit, the power of my Spirit and the light of my love will dispel it, but it will not leave voids for the enemy to take root. You see, I will fill those voids with my Spirit so that you will know that you lack nothing.

I am raising up a holy people. People that will be filled with boldness, grace and strength. People who will be anointed to take the truth into their homes, their families, their neighborhoods, their parishes … yes, even out into the world. Do not compromise your faith. There's enough of that in the world with the enemy and all his dominion who try to sow seeds of dissension, evil, lies … but I am the truth. As you keep your eyes and mind and heart set on me, I will lead you into the path of truth.

Speak out … speak out … speak in holy boldness but always in love and sensitivity. Many around you will hold their ears because they do not want to hear the truth for it will be easier for them just to abide with all those who fall away. They think they preserve their lives, their reputation, their families. They spare themselves embarrassment, but I tell you nothing could be further from the truth. The reality is, again, I am the way, the truth and I alone am life, and I am eternal. I am the eternal Now. So be of strong courage. Place your hope, your faith and your trust in me and sow seeds of love, of mercy, forgiveness, truth, joy. This will counteract fear, anxiety and confusion. Stand steadfast and remain in me and I will remain in you. I will not leave you nor forsake you. Do not compromise your faith.

    It is the truth that I have established on earth, my Church … my one, holy, catholic and apostolic Church. The magisterium safeguards the rich deposit of faith that has been handed down to the apostles and remains to this day through my vicar on earth. I will bring all to the fullness of this truth. I am in the midst and working in it and the fire of my Spirit will go out, and the warmth of my Spirit in you will draw others to me. It is through me that every one on earth takes their name, takes their humanity. I am the eternal Now. Remain in me now, steadfast and uncompromising.

3/12/15

    My Spirit is being poured out anew, poured out afresh on all the world, and as my Spirit goes forth it brings grace to heal families that have been broken, to strengthen and heal marriages, to heal family relationships. My Spirit goes forth to bring health and healing into the world that is in so desperate need of light, the light that comes from me, the only light that can dispel the darkness in the world. I send out my Spirit upon all those who believe, all those who believe in the truth of the Trinity, the truth of your one, holy, catholic and apostolic Church that I myself have instituted. Yes indeed, I am pouring out my Spirit bringing all my sons and daughters together so that once again there will be one fold and one shepherd. I wish that all would come to know the fullness of the truth. My Spirit goes forth to do a mighty work in the world.

I speak through my people. I speak through my Holy word that is sharper than any two-edged sword could be, and it cuts right into the heart and soul of all who have ears to hear and believe. I have told you that this is an urgent time. I repeat it again, it is indeed an urgent time, that is why I am pouring out my mercy. I have blessed each of you with the truth and I call you to take the truth, and not only keep it to yourself, but to share it, share it with others who do not know the fullness of truth. I am the beginning and the end, the alpha and the omega.

I call you to pray and stand in the gap for your priests who are being persecuted. I call you to stand in the gap to pray for your brothers and sisters all over the world. These brothers and sisters who have the opportunity to deny me and save their life, and yet they are filled with holy boldness and grace and strength and courage. For what would it do them to deny me and loose their life? But they have chosen the better part, but they have not died and they live forever with me in paradise.

This world is temporary. All healing is temporary, and so I call you to do the work that I have given to you to build up the kingdom of God. Reach out in love and welcome. Take care of those that you know are in need. You see, you are my helping hands. You are my loving touch. You are my forgiveness and my mercy on earth when I flow through your hands, through your heart, through your lips. Stand firm and stand in the gap. Again, I call you to pray for your priests so that they might remain firm in a time of great suffering, that they will be filled and opened to receive through the power of my Spirit, wisdom and knowledge and holy boldness.

    You are my warriors and I have armed you with the sword of the Spirit and with the weapon of the rosary. You have all you need. Do not worry or be afraid for I go before you and I surround you with a bastion of angels. Go therefore, and proclaim the good news that Jesus Christ is Lord over every trial and every situation. Proclaim the truth that I am Lord over every problem and what Satan would use for evil, I assure you I will turn for good. Fear is useless. What is needed is trust. Do not be incapacitated by fear and anxiety. You have all you need, you are fully equipped, because I abide in you and work through you. You are my beloved.

3/26/15

    I would have you remember and come to a full realization of this truth of my precious body and blood. *(A prayer group member had just praised Jesus for the gift of the Eucharist).* I would have you understand that at every Mass, every single Mass all over the world, no matter the time it's celebrated, I would have you remember that it is indeed celebrated, not reenacted, and as the Eucharist is celebrated, I would have you remember that I am the eternal God outside of time and space and that every time a Mass is celebrated I myself, yes, I myself am the priest and the victim. I myself am offering myself to the Father for each and every one of you for all generations. I did it once and for all and at every Mass, make no mistake about it, at every single Mass that's celebrated, you are brought to the foot of Calvary. I am the eternal One. I am the eternal Now, and I look from the cross for all generations that you count and I cry out, "Forgive them Father for they know not what they've done", and oceans of mercy flow out through all generations.

This is a time, a time such as this that each one of you are called, blessed, anointed and filled with the power of my Holy Spirit for there is a great work to be done. I ask you to remember that I have not left you orphaned and never will I leave you orphaned. I leave you the sacramental life of the Church to feed you and nourish you with my own life in the Eucharist, to forgive you, to heal your heart, to unbind you, to fill you with grace upon grace, to wash you clean in the sacrament of confession. I have left you the sacramental life of the Church so you will not collapse on the way home to eternal life. This is a great time. All humanity, all humanity will be put in a place and a time where a choice must be made: eternal light or eternal darkness, eternal death or eternal life. And I would have you go, I would have you speak my word more by your actions and the way you live your life than any words that would come forth from your mouth ... but speak too. Speak of my divine life, my mercy. Speak of the urgent time.

I have sent my mother time and time again, more now than ever before, and she brings a message of my love and my mercy for these times, the Eucharist ... my body, my blood, my soul, my divinity. My mother ... I am flesh of her flesh and bone of her bone. I have received this flesh from my mother. She is mother of the Eucharist. Let this word go forth for this is healing, this is deliverance, this is grace upon grace. It is the reign of my mercy. Now is the hour.

4/9/15

My people, I call you not to look at yourselves as victims, but I ask you to look at yourselves as victorious. You see, I was the only perfect sacrifice and victim, and I offered myself completely and fully for you so that you would be victorious. I won for you salvation. It cost me everything, but I paid the price in full. I paid it for each and every one of you. I paid it for all those that went before you and all those that will still come. And at every sacrifice of the Mass you are brought right to Calvary. I am victory itself. I am the beginning and the end. I am your all in all. I would have you remember that apart from me you can bear no fruit that will last, but with me and through me, miracle after miracle can happen. I not only gave you victory, I gave you forgiveness, mercy and power, and the gift of my unconditional love. I love you when you're broken. I'm close to you, close to all those who are brokenhearted. But I would have you remember that in your brokenness, I alone can put you back together. I alone am full of mercy, forgiveness and love itself.

I have a work for each of you to do and that's why I had to suffer and to die and raise so that you too could rise with me. I want you to be an "Easter" people from your head to your toes. I want you to be an "Alleluia" people. I want all who see you see the joy of Easter in you. It was not the nails that kept me to the cross. I assure you it was love, love for all. This is a time of divine mercy. It is an urgent time and I would not have you dismayed or filled with fear or anxiety for I am a God of mercy and love. My will is being worked out and accomplished, but just as with the apostles, I revealed more and more as they walked with me, as they followed me. As they became one with me, I revealed more and more of myself. They would never had believed if they recognized me. You see, it was recognizing me in the breaking of the bread that made them believe, made them know. As I broke the bread they saw my wounds and they knew and understood that I am. And so I say to you, it is in the breaking of the bread that you will not only recognize me more and more deeply in your lives, but it is in the breaking of the bread when I will feed you and nourish you and strengthen you with my own life through the sacrifice of my own body and blood. Through that meal I will feed you and nourish you and strengthen you for all that will come to pass for all of you, every single one of you, you are over-comers when you place your hope and trust in me. I love you with an everlasting love.

If I have loved you enough to lay down my life, if I loved you enough to go to the destination that I was born to go, to the cross, do you think I will not watch over you and take care of you, heal your wounds, bind them up, give you grace and strength for your journey, and not only you but your whole household.

Do not look to the past. Do not allow Satan to rob you of peace. He would remind you of every sin you ever committed, but in my divine mercy and love, I will wash you clean when you come to receive sacramental grace. He is a liar and a deceiver. He sprinkles truth so that you would be tempted to believe, but I alone am the way, the truth and the life. Come and follow me. I am all wisdom, the very seed of wisdom and I am all truth and my truth will set you free.

4/30/15

I want to rekindle within you the fire of my love. I want you to know that I am in the midst of relighting that fire. I myself am fanning that flame that is dim, but I told you that a smoldering wick I will not crush. Instead, I speak to your heart this night to remind you that I will never leave you nor forsake you. I will touch your mind and enlighten it with truth. I will touch your heart and fill it with compassion and my mercy. I will renew you in the Spirit of my love. I bring you to a new place at a new time for the new working of my Spirit within you.

There are no coincidences. It is always I working everything together to accomplish my work and my plan in you and through you when you are open to grace. I will speak new things to your heart. I will assuage the wounds of your heart. I will bring you new life. Everything else is temporary in this life, but my light, my love, my word ... eternal. I AM and because I AM, you are. I will bring you to a new place that you might grow into all that I call you to be. Have I not broken the chains that have held you bound in the past? Have I not taken away your fear and anxiety? Have I not renewed you? I will have my way. I ask you only to surrender and allow me to move in you and through you.

I am a God who forgives and I am a loving God, a merciful God, a compassionate God, but I assure you at the same time I am an all powerful God. I can raise the dead. I can bring sight to the blind and for those who can not hear I can bring hearing to them. I can open their ears, their eyes, their heart. I will bring new life, will you receive it? Will you trust me to give you eternal life? Will you trust me to work in the lives of your loved ones or do you really think you can save them on your own? I assure you there is no salvation apart from me ... the Father, the Son and our Holy Spirit. I come in power and might. I am the same God as Father and Son ... I am Holy Spirit ... one God, three persons, to bring salvation to the world.

Now is the hour, now is the time. If you hear my voice now, be prepared that I will work in you and through you in ways that you have not yet understood, for I see your heart, your heart is set on me, although you did not recognize me as Lord and Savior. You loved me when you knew me not and so I will bring you, I will bring you to the full realization that apart from me you can bear no fruit that will last. Trust me. Allow me to renew you in mind, body and spirit.

5/7/15

You see, in loving you, I give you an example how to love others. In loving you, I show you the way to love as I have loved you. You've heard it said, I love my disciples to the end, I love my apostles to the end. I love you ... imagine ... I love you with all my heart, my sacred heart. I could never love you more because I love you completely. There's nothing you could do that would make me love you more because I love you completely and unconditionally. And I have tried to show you how you should love, and yet time and time again you bicker with one another. You speak words that tear each other down and it wounds my heart. You see, I want you to speak words that will build others up. I want you to see me in others, for when you no longer look at their faults and their failings then you will see me within them and when you look I will be reflected back to you. I have loved you unconditionally. I have loved you completely. There is no way that I could give more to you than I have because I have given you all. I've given you everything that is right for each of you. I love you completely and I call you to love others that way.

The cross in all of your lives regardless of how those crosses are manifested ... those crosses come when your will crosses with my will. You see, they're the crosses that I call you to embrace because they're moments of grace. When you do for another even when you don't feel like it but you know it's the right thing to do ... do it. When you don't feel like forgiving ... forgive anyway. I have tried to show you time and time again the way I have forgiven each of you over and over and over again. And because I have forgiven you over and over again, because I have loved you in spite of your weaknesses, in spite of your sinfulness, in spite of your lack of love, I still have loved you completely. And so I say to you, the crosses that are in your lives when your will crosses with my will, yield to my will especially in dealing with your family and your friends, especially forgive even if you do not feel forgiveness, make an act of the will. I will bless you mightily and you will grow more perfectly into my likeness and my image. I have shown you the way. I have beckoned to each of you to come and follow me. Imitate me. Do what you have seen me do. Speak the words you have heard me speak. Love how you have seen me love, and the only way you can do that is by allowing my power to be released within you through my Spirit. You see, it's not a "power" that lies within you. It is your God who gives you power to love as I have loved you. Know this and forget it not.

When you find yourself bickering with one another, with your mates, with your friends, with those in your work and those in your life, those who I have placed in your life who rub you the wrong way or their weaknesses annoy you, never forget that your weaknesses annoy them too. And never forget this: all your weaknesses and all your annoying habits and behavior ... I always want to forgive, to instill grace and peace and strength and courage within your heart and your mind and your spirit so that you will reflect me more fully. You will be alive in me. You will be a light shining brightly and a fire ablaze among the earth. So these little bickerings, these little crosses in your lives, take them as moments of grace and allow me to fill you with grace so that you can overcome, so that you will not be victims but victorious.

5/28/15

You see, I call each and every one of you by name. I call all of you, and when I call you I send you forth. I send you as the Father has sent me to glorify Him. I have shared much with you. I have shared my heart. My wisdom and my knowledge I have imparted to you. I have shared my heart of mercy and compassion. I have given you glimpses of my wisdom and knowledge and discernment. I've done this because just as I have called you, so too I will call others, and just as I have sent you, I will send many more in my name. This is indeed a time to heed my word. This is a time to have ears to hear and a heart to receive. You see, it is by my authority that I bind up wounds. It is by my authority that I set people free. It is by my authority that I heal and make whole. It is by my authority that I call you to forgive as I have forgiven you. I could go on and on, but you know it is by my authority.

I am the God who created you. There is no other. I'm the God who has redeemed you, saved you, captured you and filled you with my love and immersed you in my love, and it is by my authority that I call each of you here. You see, I am a God of the living not of the dead. I came that you might have life and have it eternally. I came to give you peace, the peace that is in the midst of turmoil, the joy that is in the midst of sorrow. It is by my authority that everything came into being. I do not wield authority over you. I give everyone free choice. I give everyone the opportunity to choose between life and death. I've asked you to choose life that you might live, but many have chosen death and they are on the road that will lead to total darkness, emptiness, loss. But in my infinite mercy and love I send those out to grasp them out of the hand that would guide and lead them into eternal death, and I send my people out who know the truth, who know the depth of my love, my forgiveness, my mercy, who know that I am a God who loves unconditionally.

But I am the God who heals. I've said in the scriptures I am the Lord your God, your healer. I am the God who sanctifies you. I sanctify you from the inside out so that you can be all that I call you to be. I have a mighty work for you to accomplish, and you will lack nothing. I will give you everything that's necessary. I myself will lead you, guide you. I myself will grasp you by the hand and show you the way in which you are to go so that you can show others. I am the redeemer. There is no other by any other name. So I ask you to give to me this night all those that are walking in darkness that you know and love, all those who have left the Church that I instituted, all those who have wandered away from the truth because their ears were tickled. They do not know what they have left and so I send my people out to bring truth, mercy, love, so that in you they might see me as the God of the living and they will turn towards me, and I will heal them. I will hold them close to my own sacred heart. My mother herself will intercede for them daily until they yield to grace and receive the salvation that was always theirs for the taking ... the gift of salvation ... the gift of eternal life. Will you be my voice? Will you go into the world and bring the good news that Jesus Christ is Lord?

6/18/15

You hear of the ways that I move in your lives. You see that I work all things together for a greater good, and yet so many times when situations and circumstances come into your lives you're heart often times is filled with fear. I don't want you to be afraid. I want you to know that I am in all things. I am Lord over everything. I want you to know that I work every single thing together for a greater good. If you would really comprehend this truth, your hearts would be at peace, your spirit would be at rest and full of joy knowing that I am the Lord your God and that my name is above every other name. You see, my ways are not your ways. I've told you time and time again. But this night as you listened to the moving and the power of my Spirit at work, you are in awe, and indeed it is good. However, I want the extraordinary to become the ordinary ways that you expect me to work. I want you to see me. I want you to know that I am present with you, present at every moment of every day. Did I not say I will never leave you and I will never forsake you. I am Lord over all and it pleases me when my people place their hope and their trust in me.

Often times people hear the word "death" and they are filled with anxiety and fear and they tremble. You see, I have conquered death. I have truly conquered death. I am the resurrection and the life. My power is at work in your lives and the lives of others, and I want you to be aware of my presence in you, always my presence in you, working through you. I want you to know that fear is useless and what is needed is trust. Trust in my way. Trust in my will. Trust that I know the very thing that everyone needs, contrary to what you often think. You often times think you know best for many given situations, but you see, your hearts would not be troubled, you would not be filled with fear and anxiety if you really believed that I am Lord over your life and the lives of those you love, for even when things are not the way you want them to be, can you trust that my love is greater for you and for those that you love, greater than you could ever possibly imagine? I want to infuse wisdom and knowledge into you and the truth of realizing, without a doubt, that you have no reason to fear. Will you trust me? Will you trust in my divine will? Will you trust that I know what's best and that I will work it all together for the very best outcome for you and for all those that you pray for. Life is eternal. You're on a journey, all of you, and one day it will end, but your life ... that will never end. I say it again, all those who believe in me and have faith in me ... you have eternal life.

And to you I say, your loved ones are closer to you than you could even possibly imagine. They might have gone before you, but know this: they see, they pray, they love you. You have not lost them for they have found eternal life. Their lives have not ended. They have changed and your lives might have changed because of it, but they are with you and closer than you could possibly imagine.

I would not have your heart be troubled. I don't want you to be afraid. I am with you, loving you into wholeness, filling you with grace and strength and courage and hope. Continue to fight the good fight. Continue to run the good race. Continue to trust in my love, not only for you, but for your children, for all those that are even far off. I went to the cross. I died on the cross and rose again for all of you including those that have not even been born into the world yet. You see, time is for you. I am the eternal "Now." Trust, trust, and do not fear.

7/2/15

I want you to remember and never forget that my power at work in you, my abiding presence in you, is far greater than he who is in the world. I tell you tonight, be at peace. Do not be filled with anger, but be filled with holy boldness. Do not hate, but love. You see it is in my love working in you and through you that others will come and recognize that it is no longer you but me living in you that they see. They will begin to hunger and thirst for righteousness. For those who are opposed to my ways, those who have turned their back on my Holy Spirit, those who have wandered away, I do not, I say it again, I do not want them lost. That's why I am raising up my people. This is a time of great darkness in the world. You need to be a light to the nations. It is only my light that can dispel the darkness. It is a time when I am raising up holy people filled with holy boldness to be firm and stand firm in the truth, my truth. I am the truth and I alone can set people free. I can break the chains that hold people bound. Do you realize that? Do you comprehend that truth yourself? I call you to stand up and speak in love and tell the truth, in love. I call you to do as I do ... to love the sinner but hate the sin.

    The enemy is roaring like a lion. He knows his time is short and he comes with a vengeance. You see, hate will never overcome love. The greatest lies in the world, even if everybody believes them, are still lies, and my truth is what will set people free. You know, you've experienced it in your family. You have a daughter and she was dead in the spirit. You have a son and he was dead in the spirit, but through prayer, through fasting, they were snatched out of darkness and brought into my glorious light through the power of love, steadfast prayer, fasting. These are the things that changes man's heart. I want you to remember and never forget that I am a God of power and might and all things are under my control, but I give my people free will, but some have never learned the truth. It is never too late, my timing is perfect. I continue to call to those who are lost as I call to your loved ones who are lost, as I called to you when you were lost, and so too I call you to stand for truth. I call you to bring the truth into the public square.

Faith is a gift. It is not to be hidden, not to be ashamed of, not to cower under. I call you to be filled with my Holy Spirit so that you may be a voice crying out preparing the way of the Lord. Those who refuse have free choice. They condemn themselves. But you, you know the truth and I ask you to take the truth out more by how you live than even what you say. Now is the hour. If I was persecuted, if I was harried, do you think you will not be? The gospel is the truth. This life is temporary and they do not know that if they choose darkness and evil then the wages of that will be death, eternal death. But you, go out to the highways and the bi-ways. Go into your neighborhoods, your work places, your families, and let them know that Jesus Christ is Lord.

7/9/15

With the moving of the storm you saw the darkness, the lightning, the winds, the storm clouds. So much darkness came over. However, after the storm passed, you saw once again the light. You saw once again the skies that were clear. So too it is in these times. There's a great darkness and an even greater darkness coming, but I remind you this: I am the light of the world and in me there is no darkness at all, and so I remind you to rest in me. I remind you to have your being in me, walk with me and talk with me because I am always with you.

Do not fear, do not be concerned. So many are falling into anxiety and despair about the things that have come to pass, and still more will come, but I tell you truly, I am about a mighty work. Many prayers are being answered and yet so many are in fear. I am moving powerfully and just as the darkness comes the dawn will surely break through. I have said it time and time again, I am a God of mercy, a God of love, I'm also God of the living, and so I say to you to take the truth and power and authority that I have given to each and every one of you through your baptism. Take the power, take the authority, take the anointing and live out the gospel. Be concerned with my will. Be concerned about the light that shines brightly through you.

Wherever you go, I go with you and I move in you and through you. This is a time of great mercy and it is through you that I will touch your children, your families, your business associates, the people in your parish, the people in your neighborhoods. Yes, I will work in you and through you and I ask you to share with them the joy of the gospel! My words are not words of gloom and doom, my words are power and might and tenderness and love and mercy. As long as you remain in me, I will watch over you and guide you and lead you. Trust more in me than what you see coming or what you see happening. Know that I am Lord of all. Know that nothing can happen without me allowing it and working it together for a greater good. Do you trust me? Do you really trust me? Ask yourself, be honest with yourself. And if you don't, if you don't trust me then you, I'm afraid, will be one that will have anxiety and fears because you're trusting in the ways of man and in the world. Trust in me. I will safeguard you, I will safeguard your heart, your mind, your spirit and all those who belong to you. Trust me. I offer you life. I offer you light over darkness. I offer you power and I empower you to bring the joy of my word out into the world to dispel anxiety and fears and doubts and confusion. You have the truth, stand on my truth, speak my truth, and trust me.

7/16/15 (1 of 2)

Before you knew me, I knew you. I formed you. I fashioned you. I created you ... the way you look, the way you walk, the way you talk. I created you and gave you all the gifts and talents, yes, even though you're not aware of the many talents and gifts that you have. When I was creating you in secret in your mother's womb, I blessed you, I anointed you, I gifted you. I formed you. I formed you with my own hands in secret, and I knew you, and I loved you and I have a plan for you. I would call you this night to remember that I have said that I am your hope. I am the very reason for your hope. If I created you, do you not think that I can't re-create? If I created you in my likeness, in my image, do you think for one moment if you're created in my likeness, in my image, that I made a mistake? I have a plan for you. I created you for "now", for this very time, and I fashioned you and molded you into who you are today. I brought people into your life and I've removed people from your life, and those that you have loved who have handed on your own faith ... they're with me now ... the faith that was handed down to you.

But I ask you tonight, will you receive that gift of salvation, the gift of faith, the gift of hope, the gift of my love, the gift of my mercy? It is within you and only you to make that decision. I have loved you with an everlasting love. I will always love you, I have always loved you, and nothing you can say or do will detract from that love. I love you completely and I did fashion you. I decided on the color of your eyes and your hair. I decided what you needed within you so that you would succeed. Your personality brought me joy before you ever breathed a breath in this life. You're mine. I loved you first. You're mine, but I give you the choice ... am I yours? Freely I give you love, salvation and free will. You are mine and I will love you in all times, in all seasons. I will never forget my own.

7/16/15   (2 of 2)

I will make you a fisher of men. You have given up on yourself in many ways but I tell you that you have no idea of the plans I have for you. You will be a son of light and your witness will be a witness to many to come and follow me for I have a plan for you, a plan to prosper you, a plan to bless you and to give you a gift, the gift of peace, my peace, that the world will never be able to rob you of. I have a plan for you. I ask you this night to receive, to believe, to trust and to be obedient to my word.

7/23/15

I've called you by name, again, by name I have called you. I would not have you be concerned about those whose names you feel have been called and have failed to answer and respond to my call. I am a patient, loving and merciful God. I am slow to anger.

You responded when I called your name and that is something to rejoice over. You had ears and you heard, you had eyes and we looked at each other and you fell in love for you knew I knew you, everything about you. You knew I knew your weaknesses and your faults and your failings and you knew that I loved you through it all. You see, when I looked at you it was not I who changed, but you. When I look into the eyes of my children, it again, it is not I that change, for "I AM", but it is my love reflected in their eyes and they not so much change as they become who they're really called to be.

Like an onion being peeled away, many times pain and tears are shed. Just like a great skilled surgeon, to get to the affected area, to get to the very core of the problem, many times I have to go deep, and as a skilled surgeon will tell you, there is always pain in recuperation. There is pain in recovering, but once recovered there is a joy that goes beyond all human understanding because there is a freedom to be you, not to put on a face for your family, your friends, people that you live with and work with and know, but the freedom to be you without a mask. You see, I have created you to be all that I call you to be. You lack nothing.

And so I say to you, for those you feel have been called as well, do not give up hope. I am their hope as well as yours. I ask only that you would remain faithful. I ask that you would continue to reflect my love and my mercy, my grace, my strength and my power in your lives and that will do more than any book, any word can do to reach their hearts because you're authentic and it is only my word that can set people free. And so I ask you to guard your heart, your mind and your spirit to stand firm in this new life that I have given to each of you and to continue to fight the good fight, just don't shadow box, but fight the good fight for I tell you your reward will be great.

I say do not give up and do not loose hope in those who you want to walk with you on this journey called "life". Do you think that you love them more than I do? I went to the cross for them. I give them free choice just as I gave you free choice. The choice must be theirs.

You see, that's what love is all about ... freedom. I ask you to continue to be a witness. I ask you to continue to be a light shining brightly in the darkness. And I say to you, stand in the gap for those who do not know me, for those who do not love me, and for those who do not seek me, that through your prayers they will begin to search and through my grace, through my grace washing over them, renewing them, healing them, delivering them, they too will be set free. They too will become my disciples.

7/30/15

Am I not love and mercy itself? You have been blessed, you have been blessed because your eyes are opened to see and your ears are opened to hear the truth that has set you free. I told you I will never leave you nor forsake you. I will never abandon you. Is my love not enough for you? Am I not enough for you? You see, I have more than you can ever possibly imagine and I want to give you all these wonderful good things. I want to teach you to grow in virtue and wisdom and knowledge and grace and strength. You can not really understand the depth of my love for you, but I tell you I am the same yesterday and forever. Do not complicate me. I am a God of simplicity, a God of love, a God of mercy. As I said, I am love and mercy itself. I would gather all of my people close to my own heart. Just as the story of the pelican, did I not have my own heart pierced? As a pelican feeds its young by piercing its own heart and giving the food to the young, my heart was pierced and blood and water gushed out. If only people began to really understand that truth that my heart was pierced for you, that my blood was shed for you so that I could feed you and nourish you out of the blood that pours out of my own heart. No one could love you as I love you. No one knows you better than I know you, and loves you still.

I want you to teach others to love as I have loved you, to forgive as I have forgiven you, to be merciful as you have received mercy. I call you to be a light to the nations. I call you to be a witness of the great love, the love of my heart, the love that had the heart pierced to feed and nourish each and every one of you and all of my children. If only they knew the truth and had not walked away. And so I must send you out as my laborers because on you the word has taken root, the word was made flesh in you. I not only feed you and nourish you but I form you and fashion you and mold you into all that I call you to be.

Go therefore, and make disciples. Show your brothers and your sisters that, yes, I am a merciful and loving God. But I chastise those I love. I hold accountable those that I love. Make no mistake about it, mercy is not just a nice feeling to receive or to give. mercy is the outpouring of my heart into the hearts of others to forgive, to bind up wounds, to heal, to correct and to admonish in love, in mercy, so that you can grow into all that I call you to be and not only you but all those who will come to me through you. Am I not enough for the world? Did I not pay the ultimate price for all those, all my creatures, and yet not all received that gift of salvation. But again, I gave all free choice. So I call you out, I call you out to go and bear much fruit that as you are fed you will feed others, as you are nurtured you will nurture others, as you are forgiven, time and time again, I call you then to forgive others time and time again. So go therefore and proclaim the good news, I paid the ultimate price, paid it in full. They need only to choose life that they might live and live it in abundance.

8/6/15

You see, I work in you and through you for my good pleasure because I want you to grow into all that I call you to be. I want you to grow into the man and woman that I created you to be. If I loved you enough to be beaten and tortured and suffer such a horrific passion and then go beyond and lay down my life for you on the cross crying out, crying out on the way to the cross, "Take this cup from me, but not my will but Thine be done", there was a greater good to come out of it was there not? You see, through my death came resurrection and through my passion and death and resurrection came your salvation.

And so, often times, you miss me in the center of your lives, you miss my power, you miss my will, and so I say to you, I am the God who shares wisdom and knowledge and power. I share my power, my love, my grace, my mercy, my strength and on and on, with you. I am the God of providence. I share what I have that you might share it with others. And because I went to the cross, in your place I might add, yes, because I went to the cross for each and every one of you, I give you new life. I would have you live it in abundance in the midst of trials and tribulations, in the midst of joy and celebration. I call you to live and live life in abundance that my joy might be complete in you. Because I went to the cross I live now in every tabernacle all over the world. I left you the gift of my own precious body and blood. This is a true gift. This is the true bread from heaven. You see, I will be with you always at every moment of every day, all you have to do is avail yourselves to the gift. I give you this gift that you might have my life, that you might have my joy, and that my joy would be complete in you. Remember I have just told you, I call you to be as cunning as a serpent but as gentle as a dove.

      My people die and are being destroyed for lack of knowledge, but you, you who I set apart, I give you wisdom and knowledge and grace and understanding. I give you so much more than you're even ready to receive. I wait, I wait for you to come and to be open and to see me in the midst of all that's going on in your life. I wait till you see me with spiritual eyes. I wait that you come only asking that you might come to know me and love me and serve me ever more, and I anoint you, I bless you till your cup runs over. This is my plan that you might have my joy, that you might know the joy of the gospel, that you might be a people of joy and a people of hope.

I come to each of you in many different ways. I am the same yesterday, today and forever but I call you to grow from yesterday more fully into today and continue through all tomorrows. Remember, I am the eternal "Now", the eternal "Now". It's never too late to come to me, all things are now. I ask you to trust me. I ask you to place your hope in me. I am a God of mercy and all hope. Look for me and you will find me in the ordinary and the extraordinary and then take that message, take it out to all those that I bring into your life and know, know that I love you enough to die for you that you might have life and have it to the full.

8/13/15

What are you holding on to? What are you afraid to let go of? Are you holding on to your fears or your doubts? Are you holding on to your anxieties? Are you holding on to the weaknesses and sins? If you are, then give them to me this night for I have come that you would be free. I have come to take your burdens upon me. I have come to give you freedom and peace. Yes, you can have my peace even in the midst of the turmoil that's going on around you. I give you peace in the middle of difficult and trying circumstances. I give you my peace, a peace that is not of this world, and I have told you in my Holy word that when you keep your mind and heart set on me, I give you this peace that the world can not rob you of, that's why I am the King of Peace, the Prince of Peace, the Giver of Peace.

And I call you to bring this peace to others. I call you to recognize the gifts that you have been given, but like all gifts, if you do not use them you may loose them. As I call you to come and to seek my will over your will, it is a difficult journey to do so, and that's why I tell you to be patient with others who are struggling, that's why I tell you to be compassionate with your children, your mates, your family members, your priests, your religious, your teachers, all those in authority ... be patient, for all who seek me with a sincere heart, I will work in their hearts, I will work in their mind, I will bring the joy of my salvation to them. I will do it through you and through others who say, "Here I am, send me." There is an urgency to this time, make no mistake about it, and so I teach you, I train you, I empower you, I anoint you, I strengthen you in your weaknesses so that all who would see you would see me and in your weakness my power is at its greatest strength.

And I ask you, what do you hold on to? I want to free you up. I want to set you free. I want to lessen your burden. I want the joy of your salvation to well up within you. In these tumultuous times, peace will be your guide. You will know me by my fruits, by the peace I will give you in the midst of suffering and trying circumstances. You will know me by my fruits, they can not be counterfeited.

9/10/15

I have a plan for your life, a plan that you have never conceived, a plan that you have never felt that could be for you, a plan that comes from my heart to your heart, a plan to bless you not only spiritually but physically, emotionally, mentally. I want to touch you and give you the peace that you've tried to find in all the wrong places, a peace that lasts for a moment, a night, a week. You see, the peace I seek to give you is the peace that can never be disturbed. It is my peace, my peace I give you. Just as I breathed upon the Apostles in the upper room, they were cowering, they were filled with anxiety and fear and doubt, and their mind was filled with so many questions, but you see, I breathed on them and when I did I gave them my peace. I said it was not as the world gives peace but it was my peace I had given them, and once they received that peace, and it was a decision to "receive", once they received that peace, they were open for me to move in them and through them to accomplish miracles, to accomplish the healing of the blind, the deaf, the mute, the crippled. You see, I came to bring health and healing. I came to renew the face of the earth even in the midst of such a hard-hearted people. My work is not done and I tell you that you, you I call to partake of this work. I call you to partake of the work that I would have you do for the up-building of the kingdom of God.

You feel you have no gifts, and if you do have gifts they're very little ones, but this is not so. I have gifted you and blessed you and I have called you. I've blessed your words. I place my thoughts in your mind. I place my love in your heart and I called to you, "Come, come and follow me", and you responded to the invitation and you received grace upon grace, but now I'm about to do a new thing. Now I'm about to move in your life in a new way. I have called you by name. I'm sending you out, sending you out in such a way that others will know that you are filled with my Spirit, anointed by my Spirit. I have placed you in a place where you can grow, where you have learned, where your faith has deepened. And so I say, I have a new work that I will do in you and through you, and not only in you but in all those that you have prayed for. I have seen the tears that have been shed. I have felt your anxiety, your fears and your doubts, but now I give you a gift, a gift of hope. I am your hope. I give you a gift of trust for as you place your hope and trust in me, I will not only work in you and through you, but I will reach out and touch others that you are worried about, others that you feel do not know me, do not love me, do not believe in me. I am sending a fire on the earth, a fire of my Spirit. Be assured, do not doubt that this shall come to pass. Trust in me. Hope in me. Come and follow me.

9/17/15

You know, you are mine, each and every one of you. I love you with an all-encompassing love. I formed you, I fashioned you. I placed your personality deep within your soul. I formed your eyes, your nose, your mouth. I formed you into my likeness and my image and I continue to form you and transform you as my children. A child never outgrows the need and love of their parents. And so remember, I who created you, I who fashioned you, I who dwell within you, watch over you and protect you, I who guide you and lead you … I lead you through the snares, I lead you through the detours, and where there are great stumbling blocks, I raise you above them to step upon them as if they were stepping stones.

You're mine. I paid the price for each and every one of you. I paid it in full. I want you to realize that my Father called you into being. You were in His thought, in His heart before you were even in your mother's womb. He loved you enough to offer my life for your life and not only your life but the lives of all. Some receive that great gift and others refuse it, but I continue to watch over my children. I continue to guide you and lead you. I continue to speak to you and I want you to know that I enjoy you. I enjoy you, I will say it again. If you think that you enjoy your children when they were born, when they were babies totally dependent on you, and as they grew into toddlers and children and teenagers and young adults, oh, they seemed like they didn't need you and at one point they went on their way and were convinced they knew better, and I look and I watch and I smile, for you do the very same thing with me. Often times you think you know better. You think your way is better than my way but I tell you again, I go before you and prepare your way. I care for every single need that you have. I am a tender, merciful, loving God and I would have you know that all the times that you think you can go it alone you wind up on the wrong road or you wind up making it half-way because never can you get there on your own. You can't reach your goals on your own. You can't accomplish the good on your own, and so you turn back to me waiting for me to help you, to lead you, to direct you, to strengthen you, to lift you up when you fall down and to caress you and hold you close to my own heart when you're suffering or in pain or sick. I will never forget you. I have loved you with an everlasting love and I will continue to walk with you and talk with you. I will continue to transform you as you open your mind and heart and spirit to me. You see, you will not outgrow your need for your loving Father and I'm always there waiting for you to recognize and come to me and spend some time with me. I cherish these times and moments that you call to me and I come to you. I cherish the times that you're in the midst of temptation and you call out and I give you a way out as I said I always would. You are mine and I take care of my own.

    In the days ahead, there will be much, I say it again, there will be much havoc, trials, darkness. But you are children of the light. You have nothing to fear for my perfect love casts out all fear. Do not be concerned with the evil one for I fight the battle for you and I have overcome. Do not cede territory to the evil one. Claim all that you've ceded, claim it back, for my power, my grace and my strength are at work in you and no one or no thing will snatch anyone out of my hand.

10/8/15 (1 of 2)

    I want to exhort you … I want to exhort each and every one of you to pick up your cross and come and follow me. You see, it is through the cross and the cross alone that you have been redeemed. Each one that embraces the cross receives power from on high, my power, the power of my Holy Spirit working in you and through you to bring light into darkness, to bring joy into sorrow, to bring healing into sickness, to bring wisdom and clarity in the midst of confusion. To each of you I say do not, do not stifle the Spirit of God at work in you. It is only through my Holy Spirit and through my Spirit alone that can enable you to go out into the world, into your families, into your neighborhoods, into your parishes, and bring the light that dwells within you, my light, to dispel the darkness.

    I want you to begin to understand the tremendous gift of power, the tremendous gift of mercy, the tremendous gift of unconditional love that I want everyone to experience. Am I not the God of the impossible? Why do you doubt? Why do you feel that you're not worthy enough, holy enough, good enough? You are good enough that I came to lay down my life for you. You are good enough that I came to be crucified for you, that I gave my life for your life. Do you think that I will not walk with you on this journey of life? Do you not think for one moment, not for one moment, that I will not move in you and speak through you and use you when you are open, when you allow me to live and move and have being in you? There are many who do not know, who do not believe, who do not love me. But I say to you who do love me, who do know me, who do believe in me … I have a work for you to do. You see, it is my light in you that will dispel the darkness in the world. This is the time that each of you must take your stand and stand in the gap, bridge the gap that is such an abyss where people do not know how to come back because they have walked so far away. Stand in the gap for those who have walked away from the Church, their marriages, their families. Stand in the gap for many of my priests who are confused. Pray for them. Pray that they might be open to the fullness of the power of my Holy Spirit at work in them, that they might come to realize the gifts they have in this consecrated life of priesthood. Pray for your priests, pray for your priests daily that indeed they might remain full of holy boldness to stand the test.

    I did not promise you, never once, that you would live on "Easy Street". What I did promise you is that I would never leave you nor forsake you. What I did promise you is that I would be in you and through you at every moment in every day in the power of my Spirit. I will never leave you. I will never forsake you. I hold you close to my own sacred heart.

    If you could see at every Mass my mother standing right next to me, the angels that flood the sanctuary. If you could have eyes to see, ears to hear and a heart to understand the power of the Mass you would truly be crawling on your hands and knees, you would truly be visiting me every day in adoration. You would be in awe of my love. You would weep of how much I love you and you would indeed pray unceasingly for my consecrated sons that they would remain faithful and true in difficult times and challenges to lead my people, to guide my people into the fullness of truth so that all could stand in the gap for all those who do not know, do not believe, do not trust and do not love me. This is the message I bring to you … to trust in my unconditional love and mercy, not only in your life, but to be instruments in the lives of those who are on the road to perdition. Let my light shine brightly through you. Allow me to use you. Allow me to work in you and through you. Stand in the gap. Be a bridge so others find their way home. Do this for me and you will be blessed abundantly. Trust me. Place your hope in me. I alone am your hope, never forget it.

10/8/15 (2 of 2)

I have said this on many occasions and I say it to you this night: Come away to a quiet place and allow me to speak to your heart, comfort your soul, give you peace where there is turmoil, love you into wholeness. Allow me to move in you to forgive even the unforgivable. Come away to a quiet place away from the noise, away from the havoc of the world, away to be with me that I might speak to your heart, that I might fill you with my love from head to toe. I want to be your all in all. You say you do not hear and you want to hear. Come to a quiet place and know that I am God.

10/15/15

I would not have your heart troubled. I would not have it troubled by the things of this world that come against you. Did I not myself say to my vicar, to Peter, that Satan would sift him like wheat? And so I say it to you, your heart is so troubled because you depend and rely on your own willpower, your own strength, when in fact, it is these times that you realize that apart from me you can bear no fruit that will last. You've been sifted. Satan sifts and sifts like wheat. He finds your most vulnerable places, your weaknesses. Even though you feel strong and feel you do not have any, you go off under your own power without relying on me, without trusting in me. But I say to you, when you do this you will fall. You will fall into the weaknesses. You will fall into the shadows.

But you see, I have called you by name. You are mine and you belong to me. And so I worked this together that you might see that as strong as you think you are in your faith, you see now your weaknesses. It is through these weaknesses that my power shines forth when you turn to me, when you trust in me. I would not have your heart troubled. I would not have you grieve. I would not have you wounded. I am the one that loves you into wholeness. I am the one who molds you and transforms you into all that I call you to be, but when you step out on your own thinking "I surely will not fall, I am walking with the Lord", it is sometimes so easy to fall when you trust in yourself rather than say, "I am weak, but in Him I will be strong".

So this night I heal your heart. This night I remind you that I alone am your strength and this night I will place a new song in your heart to take away your sorrow, to take away your sadness, and to take away your guilt. I call you to be free in me and I call you to go and to be reconciled so I who am your comforter might fill you again with power and grace from on high, my forgiveness, my love and my mercy.

12/3/15

You always think that if you do not feel me, I am not present, and nothing could be further from the truth. You well know that love is not a feeling. Love is a decision. When I went to the cross for each of you it was my "yes", it was a surrender, it was loving you enough that I did not intend to ever go back to my Father without providing a way to bring you with me. Many times I move in you. I work through situations and circumstances. You do not see my hand. You do not feel my presence and yet, I solemnly assure you, that it is in these times, in the whispers of my love, in the gentle moving of my Spirit, in the prompting within your heart, that my will is accomplished. Often times it's much later when you look back and say "my God you did not abandon me". And yet until the next time comes, again you will forget that I will never leave you, that I will never forsake you.

I've called you by name. I have a plan for you and I myself will guide you and lead you, but often times you feel your way is the best way and so you do not yield to the moving of my Spirit within you. You go deep within yourself and forget that the kingdom of God is within you. You go into yourself and fail to recognize that when you turn to self instead of me you lose your peace, grace, strength, concentration. You lose your hope. And so I say to you when those thoughts come to you to take you out of the pain of the day or the moment, to take you out of the feeling of being alone or lost, misunderstood or confused, instead of entertaining those thoughts and staying in those moments I call you to distract yourself and renew your courage and send resentment far away from you, then I will come. I will come and fill you with a peace, with a grace and with strength. It'll be like in the midst of a hurricane because you have reached out to me not even realizing that I was always reaching out to you waiting. It'll be then that I will hold you close to my own heart, that I will shelter you, that I will protect you, and you will be in perfect peace in the midst of the hurricane. You will be in the "eye", the very center of it, because when you place me in the center of your life you will have peace in the midst of turmoil. You will have my strength when you are weak so that others might see me living in you and working through you. You will give them hope as they falter along the way.

    I ask you to watch and to pray. These are urgent times. These are times that are filled with so much evil, so much darkness and yes, so much evil has been let loose in the world. But you must never forget this is not a time to fear. This is not a time to shrink. This is not a time to give up. You are mine and I paid the price in full. I wrote your name in my own blood. I sacrificed all for you so that you could be where I am. You must be my voice crying out to those who are lost. The evil that comes against you are no more than fiery darts. But you, you have the breath of God within you. You have the light of the world within you. You have every single thing you need to accomplish what I call you to do. Focus on the power and love and mercy in you, working through you, and when you do the anxiety, the fears, the doubt, the confusion, it'll all be dispelled. Light always dispels the darkness.

(END OF VOLUME VIII)

Volume 9

Nihil Obstat
Rev. Msgr. Joseph G. Prior

Imprimatur
Archbishop Charles J. Chaput
Archiepiscopus Philadelphiensis
October 18, 2018

No portion of this book may be reproduced in any form without written permission from the Publisher:
Morning Star – New Dawn Ministries
P.O. Box 1446
Blue Bell, PA 19422
If unavailable in local bookstores, additional copies of this book may be purchased by writing to the Publisher at the above address.

Copyright, 2019 By Kathleen McCarthy
ALL RIGHTS RESERVED   ISBN 978-0-9641873-4-4

Artwork by Margaret M. Matt

1/7/16 *(Several people had just praised God for various miraculous physical healings that had recently occurred).*

Why does it surprise you? Why does it surprise you that I not only hear your prayers but they go up to me like incense? Why does it surprise you that I heal today as I did 2000 years ago? Am I not the God of surprises? I tell you now, there are many surprises still in store. You must expect. Have expectant faith. Am I not the divine physician? Am I not the divine healer? Am I not the very God who created those who are in need of healing? Do you think I can not recreate?

I have a purpose and a plan. I send my word to go forth and do the work it was sent to do … to bring healing, to bring deliverance, to bring peace, to bring health in minds, in bodies, in spirits. I know the plans I have for each of you. Little did you know the things that have come to pass already. But I am outside of time and space, do not look at what you see and think things are impossible. I remind you I am the God of the impossible. I remind you too that many will be called to carry their cross and share in my own suffering. I know that is hard for you to understand and sometimes even comprehend at all, but nevertheless I tell you this: For those who are willing to suffer for me, for those who carry their cross and embrace it, there are many who are being redeemed. There are many who are being snatched, snatched right out of the hands of the enemy. Remember I'm God, you're not, so I call you to trust in my ways. I call you to continue to walk in faith, hope and trust. Am I not the Lord your God? Am I not Son of the Father, son of my mother? Am I not the one who has been waited for from generation to generation? Was it not my Father who sent me into the world to be Savior, to be Lord, to be the God of mercy and love?

As you experience my healing, my love, my mercy, my power ... know as you experience that, you experience my Father and His love. Through the power of the Holy Spirit I tell you tonight, make no mistake, have ears to hear and a heart to receive this word: You shall see great and mighty works. The greatest work and the mightiest work yet is to save the souls of those who are heading into darkness, confusion and doubt. Make no mistake about it, I will save them through your prayers, through my grace, and because I am love and mercy itself.

1/21/16   *(Tomorrow is the anniversary of Roe vs. Wade)*

And I ask you to choose life that you might live. Death is eternal. Life is eternal. I call you to choose life that you might live and never die.

I want you to know that your prayers, your fasting, your acts of love and kindness and mercy come to me like incense. I tell you, I hear the cries of the innocents. I hear their cry. I hold them in my own heart. The cries resound from generation to generation. But I tell you, your prayers, the desire of your heart to save life, the desire of your heart to bring truth to deliver those in darkness, the desire of your heart to save so many of those that will perish because of the evil that has taken hold of this world ... these are days of great darkness ... but it is your faithfulness, it is your prayers, it is your works of mercy ... in the end, it is the heart of my mother that will triumph.

She weeps, she weeps for her children whose life was slaughtered. She is Sorrowful Mother. It is a dangerous thing to bring a hand against the holy innocents. That is why I call you to pray, to fast and to speak truth to dispel the evil, the darkness, the lies of the devil. He has been a destroyer and a liar from the beginning. But you know the truth. The truth has set you free. You must bring this truth to others. You are my own voice. You are my own heart. Go out into the world and bring my heart, my love, my mercy. Speak truth. A life will be saved when one hears truth and receives it, and not only their life but the child within the womb.

For those of you who have worked in the vineyard, for those of you who have spoken truth, who have sought help, who have cried out to me, you are mightily blessed and one day you will see your great reward. Do not give up. Do not loose heart. The battle is being won, and in the end, my mother's immaculate heart will triumph.

2/25/16   (1 of 2)

This Lenten journey that I call each of you on, when you begin you're full of vigor and joy and then as the time goes forth you beat yourself up for the ways that you have failed, in your mind, to do the very things you said you would do during this Lenten time whether it was internally or externally. But I would have you know just the thought that you feel bad that you fell is a gift to my heart for many never give it a second thought. But you, you are ever mindful of me in this journey.

I want you to know that as you walk along this journey I'm walking with you. I want you to know when you fall, I will pick you up, brush you off, give you new breath of the Spirit to continue on your way. This time is a time to journey forward, not to get stuck, not to be in a place that you can't move forward because you're holding on to the things behind, the things that are in the past. So I say to you now, move forward. Don't stay where you're comfortable for I'm always stretching you. I'm always calling you forward. Have I not placed you where you will grow? Have I not placed you where I have spoken to your heart, your mind and your spirit? Have I not placed you by taking you out of the world and placing you in a place that would fill your soul, your heart, your mind and your spirit with my presence? So do not think that I will leave you nor forsake you now.

You see, as you journey along this Lenten journey, it is a time of purging. It's a time of deadheading. It's a time of bringing forth new life at the end of this journey and for many that are hell bound. I am waiting to set them free where they are bound in habits that arc not conducive to a spiritual life. I will say "come out" and you will be set free. And so I say to you, as you travel along this journey I am actually loosening the bonds that hold you bound, and as you continue through the resistance of the temptations to fall back in your old ways, you will gain strength, you will gain new life, you will gain freedom through this resistance.

    I have a plan and a purpose for each and every one of you, not only you but all those who seek me with an open mind and heart. I have a plan that, as I walk along with you loosening these bonds, these wraps that hold you bound, these ties, these stumbling blocks, because you are resisting these habits, these ways that would stifle my Spirit at work in you, this resistance is growth. And when you come free, you will experience new life, a new empowerment of the Spirit, a new freedom to be you, a renewed spirit to be able to touch lives in a new way. Often times, my people, you do not even realize that you are bound up. You do not realize that you are stuck in the past or too comfortable in the present and so I call you on, I call you forth, and unless you go forward you will not experience that freedom. So when you fall, get up. I am with you. When you feel you are weak, continue forward. I am strong and will give you the strength to continue to finish the course. I want you to realize and understand that your bonds are being loosed as you move forward trusting me that I will take the wraps off. I will untie you. You will not be bound any longer and you will be a more purified, a stronger instrument in my hands and I will continue to lead you, to send you, to empower you, to love you more fully into all that I call you to be. Go forward. Let go of the past. Do not get stuck in the present but trust me and move forward.

2/25/16   (2 of 2)

Do not store up treasures for yourselves. Let me say this again, do not store up treasures for yourself. As it is written, your own life could be called home this very day. I tell you this so that you might realize that I who am all treasure, I who am perfect love will give you all that you need. I ask you to remember that all that you have comes from me because all good things come from above. Do not store up, again I say, your treasures for a later date, a later time. I alone am the Lord of all time. Use what I have given you. Be good stewards. Bless those who I have blessed you with. Bless those so they too might see the hand of God reaching out to them, that they can see that the desires of their heart I have heard and responded to. They cry out to me, "Be merciful O' God and hear my prayer". See, it is you, it is you that I use as my hands and my feet and my voice. I work through you, through all my people who "have" to bless those who "have not". So do not store up treasures for yourselves. I will give you treasures far beyond your own understanding.

Have I left you yet? Have I left you in need? Am I not the God of surprises? Am I not the one that loves you enough to die for you? Do you not think I will supply your needs and ever so much more? Trust me, trust me to work in you and through you. Know that all that you have, everything you have, your life, your family, your business, your prayer group, your parish, your friends, your children, trust it all into my most sacred heart for there they will be safe. I will tell you truly, I will not leave my people orphaned. Give all that you have to me, entrust it into my care, all the first fruits, the fruit of the Spirit. Offer me all the "firsts" and I will bless you a hundredfold.

3/3/16

How often do you recognize me in the midst of your day? How often do you think to yourself throughout the day in all the circumstances of your day: "That was the Lord, that was the Lord that did this, that was the Lord that brought it about, that was my God and His faithfulness that allowed this to happen"? Occasionally? Once in a while? Because you see, I am literally moving in your life not only daily but moment to moment. How I long for you just to think in the everyday moments of life: "That is the Lord, He's within me, moving". How many times do you say, "Thank you, Jesus", throughout the day. You see, I am always moving in you, always watching over you, never take my eyes off of you, have my angels around you to protect you, and yet, all this so many times, so many days, it's taken for granted. I want you to know that I never abandon you. I want you to know and understand that no matter where you've been, what you've done, that I am ever present, that I'm a God of mercy and love, a God of forgiveness. And day in and day out I wonder, I wonder if you really are aware of just how much I love you.

I read your thoughts. I hear your words before they even come forth from your mouth. I know all things. But yet, I say to you, do you realize, do you really understand that I am with you and my mercy is new each day, not only each morning as the scriptures say, but every moment? I have a plan for each and every one of you. I have come that you might have life. Every day I call you to come to your senses and realize the gifts, the love, the mercy, the protection, even the situations and circumstances where you plead for me to remove them from your life, you see, these may be the very ways that I call you deeper into a personal relationship with me. Will you trust me? Will you trust me to know that what is going on in your life that I am Lord over it, that what's going on in your families lives I'm Lord over it? I am Lord over every single thing.

There is no power above my power. There is no name above my name. I alone am your God and I give you the free will to receive that truth into your life that you might have life and have it to the full. I give that grace to every member of your family and to all mankind and so often I wait for them to recognize that I am in every blessing. I am in every gift. I am in every single circumstance, not only in your lives, but in the lives of all those in your families, your friends. Do not doubt ever that you or any member of your family, your friends, your acquaintances, your relatives, the people that you work with, never ever doubt that anyone is beyond my mercy and my love. My love is absolute, my mercy absolute. Trust more in me. Trust in the plan that I have for your life, and when you do I will raise you up and when those in your life, your acquaintances, your family, your friends, every one of them, when they realize that I am moving in and through them and recognize that there is no god, no god, no name, no power, no love above my name, then you will acknowledge me as Lord over your life and I will bless you mightily. I will give you gifts beyond your understanding.

As you trust in me day by day, fall that you may, I will raise you up, cleanse you, renew you and refresh you. I know every tear you ever shed as well as every tear that was ever shed of those in your lives. I want to wash away tears of sadness and grief and guilt and shame, and as I capture those tears I will fill you with living water, living water that will well up within you that will dispel any darkness, any anger, any fear, any doubt. I will give you new life that you might have it to the full. Believe this. My desire is that all of you would come to your senses day in and day out to realize, "Ahh, that was the Lord", to realize God is within mc wherever I go and whatever I do, He will never leave me nor forsake me.

3/10/16

I am doing new things, bringing about a new movement of my Spirit, doing new things in your lives. I am pouring out my Spirit in such a powerful new way that it will catch many off guard. So I tell you to guard your heart. I tell you that I am doing a new thing to bring about a new outpouring of my Spirit on all mankind. The Spirit of the living God will fall afresh and anew on many, just as at Pentecost. Out of all those who have received my Spirit through baptism ... many have just left the gifts that I have given them lay dormant within them. So I am, as I say, doing a new thing. My Spirit will fall anew upon the whole Church like a tsunami. Make no mistake about it, I will pour out my blessings, my anointings, my healing upon those who are open, upon those who are willing to be used to build up my kingdom, upon those who are willing to carry my cross, who are willing to sacrifice for the sake of saving souls and joining me in the mission. So I call you to cooperate with an outpouring of grace. I ask you to cooperate with my grace that is there to renew, to heal, to bind up wounds, to deliver, to make whole.

I have said it many times, I say it again now, the enemy is indeed roaring, prowling, seeking to destroy souls, tempting, luring, deceiving, to take my children off their path to eternal life. But you, each of you, each of you are my feet, my hands and my voice. Each of you have received an outpouring of my Spirit anew. Do not, I say it again, do not waste opportunities to offer up little sacrifices day in and day out. You see, it's in the little sacrifices often times that is the most powerful sacrifices. You see, I capture them and they add up to a powerful gift to be placed at the foot of the Altar. So I say to you, this is a time to be busy. This is a time to be active. This is the time to reach out to those who are away. This is a time for healing and restoration.

I am moving powerfully in my Church. Many think numbers are decreasing, but as I say, through the outpourings, through the tsunami of grace that will fall upon the Church, many will come, many will come to take sanctuary in the Church. This is an urgent time. My clarion call goes out. It goes out throughout the Church. Who will receive? Who will go? Who will be willing to be used? I trust that you take my word, allow it to enter into your heart and your mind and your spirit for there is a great time of mercy here and I would have you be open to it and I would have you be my instruments. I would have you, sons and daughters of the most high God, going out, reaching out, loving in my name and not judging. You see, I did not come to condemn, I came to convict. I came to grasp all those who are on the road to loosing eternal life, and so I grasp them through you. Nobody will snatch out of my hand. So commend all of your family members into my most sacred heart so that the water, the living water, would flow over them, flow over you, and bring everyone new life on the road to eternal life.

3/31/16

This is a time of new life, new birth, new joy, new experiences. Events will come forth in your life that you would never expect. This is a time of great joy, a time to be filled with the power and the anointing of my Holy Spirit who dwells within you. I tell you now that my power at work in you can do more than you could ever possibly imagine. I will take you out of the darkness and bring you into the light, and not only you, but for all those who have wandered in the dark stumbling, bumping into many stumbling blocks, people who have wandered away in the dark, people who are hiding in the dark because they do not want me to see them. Many are filled with shame and sorrow and so I say, this is a time of new life, new birthing in the spirit of my love, and new joy, a deep abiding joy that can only come through and from me. And so my power, my love, my infinite mercy will go forth through you and in you by being obedient to my holy will.

I have gifted you and I call you to use your gifts, whatever they are, to build up the kingdom of God for a greater good. My word is what lasts, all else will pass away, and so this is a time of great joy bringing the captives out of the dark into my glorious light, bringing those who have been held bound through fear, doubt, anxiety, addiction of all sorts. I tell you, now is the time to break forth from the tomb and experience the brilliance of life and my light dispelling the darkness. I choose you. I call you each by name, and to some I have a mighty work to do, but make no mistake about it, it is your gifts that will bring that work about. And so I say to you, surrender all that you have to me. Allow me to use the gifts that you have and I indeed will shine my light into the darkness for those that are hiding, wounded, broken, filled with shame and grief and doubt, filled with anger and bitterness, and so many who have lost hope completely. I am the hope for those who have no hope. I am the light for those who are in darkness. I am the joy for those who are in deep depression. I am the one who will bring new life, healing. I am the one that sets the captives free. Allow me to use you. Allow me to work in you and through you for my glory.

4/7/16

Remember, I AM … I am the One who instituted the Church and the Eucharistic mystery through the words: "This is my body". They are the words that I instituted, and I ask you to take this word out to others. I would have you know that the desire of my heart, my sacred heart, is to have those who do not know me and do not love me to come back to me with all their heart. And so I ask you to spend time, to spend time in my presence, to sit and adore me in adoration so that my healing love and power and mercy might flow from my heart to your hearts so that you can take out my love, my mercy to others.

There is an urgent need to come, to come to me with all your heart, your soul, your mind and your strength. You see, this is my clarion call. This was the word I spoke to my Son for this jubilee year of mercy. I would have you receive my precious body and blood, and as you receive me, I will well up within you, bless you, anoint you, strengthen you for this journey. I will place my thoughts in your mind and my words on your lips. I will place my love for my people in your heart. You will find yourself loving even the unlovable. As you eat my body and drink my blood you will have my life within you. And as you come away to a quiet place to be with me, to sit with me … I will love you, I will embrace you in the spirit of my love. I will envelope you. I will touch your mind and your heart and your spirit. I will give you wisdom beyond the worldly wisdom. I will give you new gifts through the power and anointing of my Spirit.

Come away with me. Visit with me. Talk to me. Look at me. Love me, for I have loved you first.

4/14/16

You know, my peace is a gift. My peace is more powerful and more pervading than all the turmoil and the circumstances that could come into your lives and the lives of all those in this world. I would remind you that I am the Prince of Peace. I would remind you that no matter the circumstances, no matter what's taking place in the world, in your country or in other countries, never ever loose this truth: I am Lord over everything. And so I would have my peace reign in your hearts regardless of what is going on in your country and your world. Even if there were cataclysmic events, my peace would still be available to you. Can you grasp that? You waste time and energy and you allow your hearts to be troubled when you are concerned with the things of the world to such a place that you loose focus. You're distracted, distracted from me, distracted from the power and the love and the mercy that is mine. Never ever doubt that the power of my peace will prevail over anything and everything that would seek to rob you of my peace … no circumstance in your lives with your families, your friends, even your enemies.

What ever is going on in the world and the events that would take place, know that I am in control and that nothing, absolutely nothing, will take place unless I allow it for a purpose and a reason. My ways, remember, are not your ways. But trust enough in me please, to know that what Satan would use for evil I would use for a greater good and that I work all things together for good for those who love me. Do not place your faith and your hope and your trust in people, in situations and circumstances, but remain in me. As you remain in me, I will remain in you and I will give you the peace that will raise you above all the turmoil, all the problems. You see, so many times you ask me to remove things from your life and they're the very things that I use to sharpen you, to sanctify you, and yes, even to heal you. Trust in me. Place your trust and hope in me, not in things, places or people, for no matter where you go I am always there. And so I call you to remain in me that I might shield you, protect you, strengthen you, heal you, renew you, and not only you but your whole household.

4/21/16

Why is it that, always and forever, my people are always looking at the things that they don't have? Why is it that they look at the things they'd like to have instead of thanking me for the blessings that they do have? Why is it that they look at other people's gifts and covet those gifts when they fail to recognize the gifts that I have given them to build up my kingdom? Why is it that my people come after their hearts are troubled, after doubts and fear and anxiety set in, rather than to turn to me in the beginning that I might give them peace. You see, peace is always my first gift to you.

Even when I came into the upper room, before I even gave a gift to my Apostles, before one word was spoken about the gifts of my Spirit, the gifts that I would give them, to watch over them and protect them and to lead them on a path to holiness, the first gift they received was my peace, my peace that I breathed on them … the breath of God. Imagine that … my breath … breathing … my breath upon them giving them the breath of my Spirit. I tell you this, that just as I breathed new life into each one of them, the new life that would take away their doubts, their anxieties and their fears, their envy, their greed, their focus of self … in spite of all those, it is my Spirit that rested upon them to give them the peace that the world and all its troubles could not rob them of or distract them from the course I had set them on. And because of this, because of open hearts and open minds within them, I was able to set a fire on the earth through the hearts of all those that they touched allowing my fire to ignite a heart, a soul, a life with the fire of my love. This is grace in action.

Don't you want to receive that grace when you're troubled, when you're failing, when you're stumbling, when you feel lost, when you're afraid, when you've been wounded, when you walk and try to hold yourself up straight, when you want to throw yourself down and cry, when you put your head up high and put a façade on that everything's fine when inside you're broken, you're hurt, you're confused? This is what I want for you … to turn to me so that I can fill you with a gift of new life through my breath upon you renewing you and refreshing you. When you are spent I breathe afresh on you and I draw you into the fire of my love. The fire then will burn away all those things that you've focused on and you stumble through, all those things that distracted you from coming to me.

Why is it that you wait so long? Why is it that you would rather suffer these things than allow me to bring you peace, grace, strength and hope. If you take care of your own family and you hurt when they hurt, how much more do you think I want to take care of you? My heart hurts. It is wounded when my people do not turn to me to receive respite, to receive the joy of my Spirit to dispel the sadness or grief, to dispel the trial and tribulation. It is sad that you wait so long every day instead of coming to me immediately so that I can alleviate and relieve your stress, your discomfort, your lack of peace.

Turn to me. Come to me. I will come as tenderly as a mother. I will come with the authority as a father and guide and direct you back on track on the road that will bring you peace and happiness, a happiness that comes deep within your being, not being happy that will be fleeting but a happiness and a joy deep within. Turn to me quickly. Let me heal your heart. Let me renew you and refresh you and give you new life, new life in my Spirit.

4/28/16

I have told you that they will know you are Christians by your love. I reiterate that from time to time. It's such a powerful truth, a truth that can set you free.

I want you to think and ponder these last several days in your week when you were talking to your mate, your children, the people that you work with, the people in your parish, the people that I bring in and out of your life on a daily basis. Would all those who have seen you in these past several days, would they wonder "Wow, I know they're Christian by their love, their love for one another". You see, the Father sent me into the world. You do not see Him but I have seen Him and I have come so that you might see me. The Father and I are one as I have said, and I have come that you might have my joy within you so that my joy will be complete in you. I have come to give you my light to dispel the darkness not only in your lives but even a little ray of light to dispel the darkness in other's lives. You are so much more capable of loving as the Father has loved me. You are so much more capable of loving unconditionally as I have loved you because I have left you my Spirit. It is only in and through my Holy Spirit that can teach you to love as I have loved you. It is only through revealing my love to you through the power of the Holy Spirit that you are able to love with mercy, that you are able to love even the unlovable in the eyes of the world. I have stretched you time and time again. I have brought you out of your comfort zone and called you to come out into the deep that I might inflame your heart to love me evermore and in doing so you will begin to love others evermore. What the world needs now is to see my love at work in the world, and when they do, their lives will change. My love in you will give them hope, when you love them in me ... that is the only way you can love the unlovable, that is the only way through the Spirit of the living God working in you and through you, that you can bring hope to the hardest and coldest of hearts. It is through my love, the love that is between me and my Father ... it's the love I give to you, the love that I pour out into your hearts.

I want you to ponder these last several days of this week and I ask you to think of the words that came forth from your mouth. Were they words to build up, to encourage? Were they words to edify and strengthen? Were they words to bring peace and consolation and hope? You see, I have loved you time and time again in the midst of your weaknesses and failings and faults and it is only because I have loved you in the midst of all that struggling, in the midst of your faults and your weaknesses and your failings that you have come to know my love, for it is only me, it is only through my Father, it is only through the power and Spirit of my love in you, my gift to you, the Spirit of the living God, it is only in that gift that you can bring my salvific love to others. Apart from me, apart from yielding to the power and promptings of my Spirit in your life, you will only bring your words, your hearts, which will bear no fruit that will last.

And so I say, ponder these days and recognize whether you are speaking my word, you are loving with my heart, you are counseling with my living word, or was it your own? You are in a place now where you have grown, where you have been stretched, where you have been challenged, and when you are challenged and stretched, it is in these times that you will rely on the power of my love at work in you. I am with you always. Others must experience that truth so they can be set free from the things that hold them bound to the world.

So allow me to love in you, console in you. Allow me to be merciful in you and also allow me to teach through you. Allow me to exhort through you. Allow me, forever and always, to speak truth in you. Often times you think others are not ready to hear it but I remind you this night it is only the truth, my truth, my living word, that will set people free.

5/12/16

I will come to you in the silence. I ask you to learn to be still. Indeed I speak to you in the silence when you shut out the rest of the noise in the world. There is much I wish to say to you and throughout your day I prompt you, I prompt you in my Spirit to be still, to take some quiet time with me. There is so much noise. There's so many distractions. There's such darkness, but a new dawn will be coming. You see, I want to give you so much more. I want you to trust me. I want you to invite me into the silence of your own hearts.

There will be much coming that could destroy your peace. There will be many things that could fill you with distress, even fear, and certainly anxiety. But those who do not take the time to listen to me, those who do not take even a few moments to come away with me to a quiet place, they will experience havoc. They will experience unrest. They will experience doubt and fear and confusion. But you, you're mine and I speak to you heart to heart and I tell you things that are beyond your understanding, but this you will understand: You have in me the greatest friend you will ever have. You have in me the peace that goes beyond all understanding. You have in me the one who abides in your soul. You have in me your redeemer. You have in me your father. You have in me the beautiful gift of my mother and you have in me the Church I instituted, this one, holy, catholic and apostolic Church. This is your safe haven. That is why I tell you to be still and allow me to speak into the depths of your heart that you might then be a light to others dispelling the fear and the anxieties and the doubt and the confusion that will come to many. I want you to trust me. You do not trust me, you know, with all that you have. You try, but you do not listen in the silence of your heart, and so you get distracted.

  Do not cede any territory to the enemy. You have ceded far too much already. Take it back. Claim them for me, your children. Claim them for me. Claim them in my name just as my Son claimed each of you in my name, the name I gave Him before the world began. I love them so much, but they too have shut me out, and so I depend on the ones that have not, to be a light in the darkness for those who have.

  Commend your business into my hands. I am the greatest business partner you will ever have. Commend to me all your undertakings. I will take each and every one of them, bless them and anoint them.

I give you the gift of my life through the gift of my Spirit dwelling in you. Do you think my Holy Spirit is an event? Is that what you're waiting for? I assure you my Holy Spirit that dwells within you is not an event, it is not a happening. My Holy Spirit within you is a person, the third person of the blessed Trinity. This is who dwells within you … the love between my Son and myself, the love so great that there is no words to express … spiration indeed, because no words can describe our love and so I showed you in the flesh that you would come to believe that no one will ever love you the way I love you because I literally sacrificed myself for each and every one of you. Some have received that redemption and others do not even give it a second thought.

So again I say to you, do not cede your friends, your families, your businesses. Do not cede territory to the evil one. Do not despair. Do not loose hope for I will empower you and through you empower others to know the truth and to be set free by the truth. So do not fear. Do not be dismayed. Do not be confused. I say this to you so that you will remember that there is nothing to fear as you remain in me and I remain in you.

5/19/16

My Spirit is always with you. My Spirit moves in you and through you and yet how often you fail to invoke my name. How often you fail to call upon me to fill you anew each day, to breath on you anew, to empower you, to fill you with the gift of my love. I created you for love, you know. I called you to really be a messenger of my love, my mercy, my forgiveness. Often times you're reluctant to forgive and yet you pray, you pray that I would forgive you as you forgive others. Do you really want me to? Do you want me to forgive you the way you forgive others? Probably not. You see, I forgive you completely. I forgive you unconditionally when you turn to me with a repentant heart. I fill you with new life. I fill you with a great grace to go, therefore, and walk in the fullness of the Spirit, to be a Christ-giver to others.

You have seen the Spirit being poured out at Pentecost by the signs and the wonders of Pentecost. You've seen a baby be baptized and you see the water being poured over the person being baptized and you are so aware of this gift of new life, however, I am the unseen guest within you, within your brothers and sisters, and every time you call to me and invoke my name I fill you again, I renew you, I give you a new infilling of my Holy Spirit that carries you from grace to grace. I fill you with my Spirit, the Spirit that empowers you, the Spirit that enables you to be all that I call you to be. I leave my Spirit with you so that you can continue on this journey of life and enter into eternal life, for you see, without me you will bear no fruit that will last. You will stumble around in the dark and be lost, so that is why I left my Spirit with you so that I could be the light shining brightly within you to be a lamp to your feet so you will not stumble, so you will not go down the wrong path, and when you seek your will over mine, and you do, I will enlighten your mind and your heart and your understanding to turn back.

Many come and ask me to heal, heal them physically, spiritually, emotionally, but very few come and ask me to heal their soul and yet many are "soul sick". And so I say to you, pray for those who have lost their way. These are urgent times. I call you to be Christ-givers. I call you to bring mercy, love and the joy of the Lord. So just as my mother went to Elizabeth and John leapt in her womb when he heard my mother's voice, so too my people, by the power of my Holy Spirit dwelling in you, living in you, sanctifying you, other's spirits will leap for joy when you announce the good news to them. Even at your presence, even when you use no words others can sense the power of my Spirit at work in his soul.

So go for me. Go out into the world. Don't wait for things to happen. Make things happen by proclaiming the gospel. Be assured that you are not alone. I am with you always. I will never leave you nor forsake you. Again I tell you, it is for a time such as this that I have called you into a deeper walk, a deeper personal relationship, a deeper love. We created you in our likeness and our image so that others might see you and believe that I am a God of the living and not of the dead.

5/26/16

You know how you love your family. You know how you want to spend time with your family, and you know that you want to be the best that you can be. You want to provide for them and take care of them. You want them to know how much you love them, not only by your words but in the many ways you manifest that love for your family. So too, it is with me. I manifest my love in many different ways for my family, the mystical body of Christ. I enlighten your mind. I give you wisdom and knowledge and understanding. I place my thoughts and ideas within your mind and with the understanding to know how to accomplish the things that you have to do. I place too my presence within each of you so that you can recognize me in the ones that I bring into your life so that you know without a doubt that I am present always.

I love my family. I love you, my sons and my daughters, and my heart rejoices when you rejoice in me. I want to give you the desires of your heart. I want to be able to walk with you and talk with you day in and day out. But I also want to take care of each and every one of your needs … emotionally, physically, spiritually. And when you are doubting or full of anxiety, I come to give you a peace that nothing can rob you of … not the things of the day, the distractions of the world. My peace is a peace that stays rooted within you and nothing will rob you of that peace when you place your hope and trust in me. You are my family. Why would it surprise you that I love you, each and every one of you, enough that I would lay down my life for you?

This night praise and thank me for the gift of your own families. Believe me, let me tell you this truth, I myself bless my family, minister to my family, supply all the needs of my family, and I give you the gift of family so that you can know me in them, but especially know me in the family of believers as you come together at the banquet table, as you come together, all of you, offering me yourselves, your problems, your sufferings, your joys and your triumphs. I am with you always.

6/2/16   (1 of 2)

Do you not realize that I have a plan for you? Have you not yet understood that I have not only a plan for you but that I will bring it about in your life, that I will guide you and lead you. I will direct you. I would set your feet firmly on the path that I want you to walk and then I myself will go before you and prepare the way.

I know you feel that you've been abandoned. I know you feel that I have not been there for you. I know often times you see my love, my presence, my mercy and my power being manifested in the lives of others and you feel that you would like to experience that. You feel that you're on the outside looking in most times. But I tell you now, I've called you by name. I fashioned you and molded you. I breathed my own life into you and called you into being because I have a plan for you, because I have loved you with an everlasting love. I comfort you when you are wounded and hurting even though you recognize me not.

I do not make mistakes. I've created each of you out of the desire of my own heart ... the way you look, the way you talk, the way you walk, the way you move, your personality, all the gifts that I placed within you. Before you were even in your mother's womb, I knew you. I want to fill you with living waters, the living water of my Spirit. I want to open the breadth and depth and height of my love for you so that you can begin to understand that I have never forsaken you nor abandoned you, that I have been with you every moment of your life even though you feel me not, even though you do not sense my presence.

You know the sun is shining. You know it's there in the sky. You know it gives light and warmth and heat. Yet on a dark, dreary, miserable day, you can not see the sun and often times you can not see the light nor feel its warmth, but just as assuredly you know it's there. That's how I have been with you. Though you feel me not, I am truly there. Though you have not felt my love and my warmth, have not felt my presence, know that my presence has touched you while you were still in your mother's womb.

You see, before all time began I called you into being. I called you to know me. I called you to love me and I called you to trust me, and so I ask you to begin anew. I ask you to step out in faith. I ask you to say "yes". I ask you to receive my love, my presence, my power in a new way in your life. The choice is yours. I am a loving God and a patient God. I am the only God. There is no other. And as you place your hope and your trust in me and begin to believe that you are precious in my sight, until then, you will not experience the joy of my Spirit. Even though I am in you, moving through you, trust is not always trusting in what you do see but faith comes by trusting in what you have not yet begun to see but believe it will come about.

6/2/16 (2 of 2)

No more than you would place yourself in a large vat of scalding water because you know it would harm your body and possibly destroy your flesh, nor would you jump into a caldron of fire because again you know that it would destroy you and take your life ... why do you put yourself in situations that could destroy your soul, wound your heart, thinking it's not going to really hurt you? But so many place themselves in situations that can wound their heart, crush their spirit, place them in knots inside, and yet not recognize that these things that they try to fill their lives with could cost them their very eternal life. These are times that you must share the truth with others. These are the times that many will follow those who tickle their ears. But you, I fill you with Godly wisdom. I fill you with my Spirit to empower you, to speak my word, and to accomplish the works that I did when I walked upon the earth, and the works that I will do through you, through the power of my Holy Spirit in you.

6/16/16   (1 of 2)

I speak to your heart this night. I want you to really ponder these words. I want you to be still. I want you to allow these words to take root into your heart, into your mind, and into your spirit. So often you look back always looking at what could have been or what should have been, and many times you wonder about the future … what will it be? I only want you to realize, because life is such a precious gift, I want you to realize that all you have is "now". The past is gone. The future has not taken place. Even tonight is not yours. You have "now".

And so I want to share with you the depth of my love for you. You lose your peace when you look everywhere but at me. You look to the past. You look to the future. You look to other people and you look at the things that they have and you wish that you had them, and so you say, "Poor me, why don't I have those things?", instead of looking at me and realizing that all that you do have comes from me. All good things come from me and I have blessed you with them.

You not only take me for granted but you take all the things in your lives for granted … the homes, the cars. You take your family members for granted. You take your friends for granted. You take your livelihoods for granted. So you see it's this innate ability to want more than you have and not to be satisfied with what you do have. I have blessed each of you, not only you but each member of your family, with so much and I have shared with you those that have so much less than you, and they are content. And so I ask you to ponder, why is that? Why are some contented with less? Why are they contented even in turmoil? Why are they at peace in the midst of all that's going on in their lives that everyone else stands back and wonders how they cope? It is because of me. It is because they look to me for their needs. They look to me for grace and strength. They look to me and place their hope and trust in me, and that is the reason they are never disappointed come what may. And when you learn this your hearts will not be troubled so easily. Will you not want to hold on and grasp tightly to all that you have for fear someone else might make use of it or take it?

So I call you to look more to me. Don't look to the past. Don't look to the future, but praise me and focus on me in the present day, in the present moment, so that you then will see all the ways, all the many ways, that I manifest myself throughout the day in your lives. So I ask you to ponder this. I ask you to be at peace with where you are and what you have and to share with those who do not have what they too wished they had. Will you do this? Will you look to me for your needs? Will you trust in me that your needs would be supplied and would you place your hope in me so that you will never be disappointed?

6/16/16 (2 of 2)

There will be much to come that will tend to fill you with anxiety or fear and these things will come quickly, but I say to you, as you place your hope and trust in me I will guide you and lead you. I will watch over you and your whole household. Am I not the God who created you and formed you? Before you were even in your mother's womb I knew you.

All things past away. Everything is temporary except my life and my love and my presence and my word. So do not look here and there for answers. Trust that I am in control and everything else is under my Lordship. I am with you. I will never leave you or forsake you. That's all you need to know … that I am with you always, and in that you can trust. In that truth you can be free from the worries of the world.

6/23/16

Why is it that you explode over small things, unimportant things? Why is it that you become so angry with those who only love you and want your best? Why is it that you rob yourself of peace because your anger is really within you? It's that anger turned inside that leads to the depression that you've experienced.

But you see, I want you to move forward. I don't want you to be stuck. I want you to be able to move forward. I want you to be able to be a light in the darkness. I want you to be able to reach out to others so they might see my great love and mercy for them in you. There are so many ways I want to use you, so many ways that I want you to bring my love and my peace to others, and you have no idea how the enemy works on you after you lose your temper, after you become angry and explosive. You see, all that could be avoided if you would place your hope and your trust in me knowing that whatever disturbs you, whatever distracts you, whatever is taking away your peace, turn to me … turn to me and I will give you light to dispel the darkness. I will give you peace to dispel the anxiety and the anger.

Listen to me. There is much I have for you to do. There are many that I wish you to bring the good news to, but when you're disgruntled, when you're filled with anger, when you explode and your temper explodes, it only causes heartache to those who are in the midst of it. It only causes you shame or guilt or anger against yourself for acting the way that you did. But you see, I see you through my eyes. I see the plan I have for you. I see all things and you let your mind run with the way you think things are, when they are not.

So tonight I send my word to bring peace into your hearts, into your minds and into your spirits. I am the Prince of Peace. I would have my people, my children, love of my heart, to be at peace. All you need, before you even speak the word, is that you turn your thought to me and I will enter in and bring you peace in the midst of that anger, peace in the midst of turmoil. You see "I AM". I am the healer. I am the Prince of Peace. Even when you think troubles wear you down, even when you think things are impossible, I remind you that all things are possible with me.

6/30/16

I did not start many churches. I did not build many churches. I instituted one Church ... one holy, catholic and apostolic Church. You must remain faithful and true in times of great hardship. Again I say to you, I only instituted One Church and this too you must stand in truth and follow her teachings. There will be much upheaval, but I call you to remember that it is the truth that will set you free. Again I tell you to remain faithful to the truth of the magisterium of your one, holy, catholic and apostolic Church regardless of the cost.

You see, it is now for a time such as this that my love and my mercy and my word must be spoken of. It is for a time such as this that I call you to labor in the vineyard. It is for a time such as this that I call you to holiness, that I've set you apart to become holy. There is absolutely nothing to fear, but there is much to be aware of, so I call you to guard your heart. There will be many splinters, but you have been redeemed by the Savior of the world on the one true cross. Let my light be a lamp to your feet. I stir up within you grace and courage and hope. You have been formed well and informed well. Others will be in need of being set free. I remind you again, that it is only my truth ... I am the way, the truth and the life ... it is my truth that will set my people free.

There is not an American Catholic Church. There is not another church that I instituted, except, the one, holy, catholic and apostolic Church ... catholic universal, in truth. For I am God, there is no other, who has loved and created mankind out of the depth of my heart. I ask you only to follow the Truth, that is how you will be safe.

Do not run after fables. Do not let your ears be tickled, but remain firm in the truth. This is the truth: I instituted <u>one</u> Church. I am pouring out my Holy Spirit to draw my people back. I am calling my people home to the one, holy, catholic and apostolic faith and Church.

7/7/16

When is the last time that you really were still and in that moment, or those moments, did you listen? Do you listen to me in those quiet moments? On the hot days and a cool breeze passes over you, do you think of me ... because I'm in the wind, I'm in the silence, I'm in moments that are lived throughout the day. The beautiful sunsets ... I created them for you, just for you, for you to view. The mountains and the seas ... created for you. I spoke and they came into being. The waters subsided and the beauty of my creation came forth. I am the master ... the master artist ... the master musician. When you hear a beautiful melody, a song that stirs your spirit, do you think of me? In the midst of tumultuous situations, in times where you feel you're surrounded by chaos and you don't know how to find peace, you don't know how to rise above it, and a moment of grace fills your heart and your soul ... do you realize that that's me? When you are confused and you don't know really what is the truth of the situation or the circumstance, do you call on me? Or when, like the rush of the Spirit, I fill you with peace, do you think of me then? When you're so busy and you have so much going on and your plate is overflowing and all of a sudden you're filled with a calm, and one by one these things are accomplished with even time left over to come back to being still, to know that I am God, do you think of me then? When you receive me in Holy Communion, do you ponder the majesty of what has happened in your life or are you looking at others? Is your mind wandering? It happens to everyone, you know, but do you take control and pull your thoughts back and contemplate me? Do you think of me then? In the moments of great joy when you've received gifts ... a gift of the Spirit, a monetary gift, a gift of friendship, a gift of new life, a gift of employment, a gift of healing balm to a broken heart ... do you realize it's me? Do you think of me then? You see, I've just recounted to you some of the ways that I am with you at all times in every moment in every day and I could go on and on and on. Basically, I ask you to ponder the thought: When do you think of me? Is it in times only when you need me when you call out to me ... when you need a prayer answered, a problem solved ... when someone is hurting or dying? Is that when you call to me?

    I wait, I wait for you. I'm always there. I wait for you to recognize me in the present moment. This is my gift to you moment to moment throughout the day. Seize the moments. Enjoy our time together. Seek me throughout the day and you will experience a peace and a joy that will flood your soul, and your heart will rejoice because you will know you and I are one. Imagine that. God and His created child ... one through the gift of my Spirit joining us together.

I've allowed you to call my Father your father. I've allowed you to have my mother as your mother. Think of me. Thank me and rejoice for the gift of the moment, for moment after moment I try to get your attention so that you will think of me for you are always in my heart and my eye is forever on you. I love you, I protect you and I flood your being with grace and I think you will begin to say, "Ah, Ha, that was the Lord", and when you do, I will bless you even more. Remember me, not only in the breaking of the bread when I feed you and nourish you and give you myself completely, but remember me for I am with you throughout the day and even in the night as you sleep I watch over you and protect you. So rejoice. Rejoice that I have never left you nor will I ever because I love you with an everlasting love.

7/14/16

So many times you feel burdened. So many times you're fatigued, exhausted, spent. So many times you feel overwhelmed with life's circumstances with all that's going on in your lives and in the world. But you see, I am the answer, not only to life's problems, I am the answer for all problems in all places for all time. I look and I see those that have grown so weary and so tiresome and I whisper to them, I call to them, just as I call to each of you, but they do not respond. They trust more in the world. They trust more in promises that people make.

Promises that are empty because they have no power, no anointing, no authority behind them ... empty promises ... things that tickle the ears ... things that entice the eyes ... things that will betray the heart. But I call, I continue to call, and when I call I ask: Do you really believe? Do you believe that I am the solution to every problem? Do you believe that I am life itself and that I have conquered death and there is nothing to fear? Do you believe that I am all goodness, mercy, the font of all love? Then why do you insist on being weighed down by holding on to the weights that you burden yourself with? For you see, regardless of what is going on in the world and regardless of the circumstances of each of your lives, I am God and you are not, and yet you fail to look to me for salvation for I want to save you from being burdened, troubled, exhausted and overwhelmed. I feel your every pain, every pain. I feel your heartache when you feel betrayed, when you feel that you are not supported, when you feel that you really don't make a difference in the lives of the people that you love.

If you only knew how much I love you. If you only knew how I wait for you to respond to my call, and not only you, but all those in the world that have closed their eyes and their ears and their mind. I ask you this night: Do you really believe? Do you really know that all things are possible with me? I have not changed. I have not changed in over Two thousand years, so I am the same yesterday, today and forever. I still heal. I still bind up wounds. I still deliver from the kingdom of darkness into the kingdom of light. I send my breath to breathe upon my people anew to renew them and to refresh them when they are weary and tired.

If only you truly would understand ... understand that I will fight the fight with you because I am victor. I will walk the walk with you to watch over you and protect you and spare you harm, and I will rejoice with you. I will fill you with my peace and my joy and then I will rejoice over you when you come to the knowledge that indeed I am the only answer, I am the only solution, I alone am the liberator. I alone am God, there is no other. I alone am the resurrection and I want to resurrect each of your lives. Many are the walking dead and I want to set them free. I want to heal them and deliver them and fill them with new life.

And to you who believe but forget to turn to me ... in all trying times, in all tumultuous circumstances, I would have you know without any inner doubt that I wait for you too. You see, I want to give you more ... more power, more grace, more strength, more joy, more love. Whatever you want, whatever is your heart's desire, I want to give you even more. I can not be out done in generosity. I am a generous giver. I am a passionate lover. So turn to me, call on me, reach for me, think of me, desire me, for all the desires of your heart I will enter into, for all your empty promises in the world, I will fulfill my promises. I came and died that you might experience life to the full and that is my promise.

So if you're weary and overwhelmed and you feel so burdened, then turn to me and I will fill you with grace and strength, and I will give you my joy and my joy will be complete in you.

8/25/16 (1 of 2)

In the days ahead there will be much turmoil, there will be confusion, anxiety, and yet you, you I call to remain at peace, firm in the belief that I am Lord over all things. I will have my way. I have a plan and my plan is going to be completed, and it is in these times that you must stay close to the one, holy, catholic and apostolic Church. It is through the Church, through my life in the Church, that you will be sustained, that you will be at peace knowing that these things are to come, and they too shall pass.

I call you to be ever mindful that all anyone has is *"now"* … that in a blink of an eye you could be called home … that in a blink of an eye things can change drastically, but know that I am Lord over all. The reason I say this, the reason I speak to your hearts is that you might be evermore mindful that it is in me and through me, it is in receiving my precious body and blood, receiving my life in you which will sustain and heal and renew and refresh. You know that you are loved. You know your Lord and your God. You have experienced my Trinitarian love and so do not be blown about from whim to whim. Do not be fooled. Do not be led astray. Do not let your hearts be troubled for I am Lord over all. I remind you of this so that you would take to heart the truth that there is one, holy, catholic and apostolic Church … one Church that I founded myself. No other church can lay claim to that.

I am bringing my people back to that truth and in the midst of this there will be chaos, but it is not a time to have you loose hope, to have you fear. It is a time such as this that many will become enlightened. It is a time such as this that many will come back to their faith. It is a time such as this that I will raise up a people to be a light in the darkness. It is a time such as this that I will continue to raise up holy priests. Priests that know the truth. Priests that will sustain you through the sacramental life of the Church. They know the power in my word. They know the life and power in the sacraments.

Let nothing tickle your ears. Do not rely on things that sound good. Rely on me, my word, my life, my grace, for it is through my word that I will guide you and go before you so you will not stumble and fall. It is by my light that I will dispel the darkness that would come against you. It is through my love and my divine mercy that much will be shaken up. But do not fear and do not be afraid, these things are bound to happen, but what people forget is that I am Lord over all and that through the power of prayer, through the mercy that I will pour out on the people, there is hope, and hope never disappoints. So do not be disturbed when you hear things that would try to rob you of my peace for you will have peace in the midst of the turmoil when you know that I am Lord over all. And the reason I say that I alone am the giver of all life, I alone am Lord over all life, and that I could call anyone home at any given moment, is to enlighten your minds and hearts to the truth that will set you free.

Be prepared. Grow in grace, wisdom and knowledge. Keep your mind and heart set on the kingdom of God and be not afraid for I am with you. Others will see this great gift of peace within you. They will see the fire of my love within you and it will start a spark in each of their hearts and they will be drawn to the living God through the fire of my love at work in them through the fire of my love at work in you. Be faithful. Do not compromise and guard your heart and allow me in, no one else, to be your focus, your strength and your life.

8/25/16   (2 of 2)

Use the gifts that have been given to you. Use the gifts to build up the body of Christ ... the gifts of love and mercy ... the gifts of wisdom and knowledge and understanding and fear of the Lord ... the gift of prudence, and all the gifts that I have given you of my Spirit. Remember this: I alone am the gift-giver. I can not be outdone in generosity.

So seek after me with a humble heart remembering and never ever forgetting that these are my gifts being manifested through you, and praise and thank me for all the ways that I work in you and through you for my glory ... the glory of the Father, the Son and the Holy Spirit.

9/1/16

I want you to remember that when I called my disciples, I sent them out two by two. There's a purpose and a plan for doing that. You heard that one Hail Mary can bring about a powerful work, and I tell you now, I tell you so that you will not forget: one Mass, one holy Mass can do more than all the people in the world praying at the same moment in the same day. If you only knew. Because every Mass, every single Mass, brings heaven and earth together. Every Mass brings Calvary forth and united with the salvation that I came to bring. I want you to become more and more aware of the power, the healing, and the merciful love that is in every single Mass that's celebrated.

I call you to pray for your priests. I call you, each of you specifically who I've called here tonight, to be the warriors, the prayer warriors, for my sons. I call them to shepherd, but I call you, each of you, to intercede and stand in the gap for they are indeed on the front lines, and the dominion of darkness, though it comes against them and many will fall, it is through your prayers, through the prayers of those who believe and know the truth that I am alive mind, body, soul and divinity on every altar and every tabernacle all over the world. And I would have you remember this, make no mistake about it: though the gates of hell will try to tear the Church down and to overcome her, this will never ever happen for the gates of hell will never prevail against my Church. But I do call you to pray for your priests that I might continue to raise up holy priests with clean hands and a pure heart. Pray for your priests. Pray for religious and pray for your brothers and sisters in the Lord who are fighting the same battle that you fight day in and day out.

You must be one in the Spirit because the Spirit of God prays in you and through you with moanings and groanings that can not be understood. These words are being prayed through the Spirit according to God's will. So pray and stand in the gap for the priests. Most especially, without the priest you will have no Eucharist which means you will not have my body, my blood, my soul, my divinity bringing you my life.

So be vigilant. Guard your heart, your mind and your spirit, and press on, press on and do not give up and do not loose hope. You are my warriors. Do not worry. Do not fear and never loose hope.

9/8/16 (1 of 3)

I want you to grow in my love. I want you to begin to understand that I love you unconditionally. I love you in ways that you can't even understand. When I look at you and I see the way you smile, the way you chuckle, the way you walk, your personality, your character ... I just want you to know that I love you so much, and when I see each of you so individually different but yet I see the thread of my love knitting you all together, it blesses my heart. Yes, it really does bless my heart.

I see you growing. I see you reaching out to others. I see your "ups" and your "downs". I see all the ways that you confide in a few chosen people about the ways that you don't understand my working. But I will tell you this: I am always working everything together for a greater good. The most important thing you need to understand is our personal relationship. You see, if you keep me in the very center of your life, if you remember that I am Lord over every single thing … I'm Lord over every thing that happens in the world even when it seems to be a horrific situation. Everything has a purpose and a reason and I work every single thing together for a greater good. I ask you to focus on your personal relationship with me. You see, as you grow in union with me, if you grow more and more in love with me, if you grow in wisdom and knowledge and understanding of who I am and who you are in me, then you will be able to do far greater things than you could have ever possibly imagined.

  You see, I have a call on your life, each of your lives. There are no accidents. It's not happenstance. Everything is a divine appointment. And those that feel that they will try to thwart my ways, those who feel they will try to draw you away, those who will try to bring anger and resentment and bitterness into your life … you must remove yourself from those situations. You see, I would have you be filled with grace and peace and strength and love because I want to send you, I want to send you to the people that I bring into your lives so that you can draw them into my heart so that I can fill them with new life.

  Many are the walking dead you know. Many look like they're happy on the outside but they're crying on the inside. Many speak that they are happy and everything is going good, but on the inside they're gripped with fear and anxiety. They're gripped with confusion and doubt. You see, it is only in me and with me and through me that I can bring light where there's darkness and peace where there's turmoil.

So I want you to know that the most important thing is the relationship between you and me. And as you build that relationship, as you talk to me, as you walk with me, as you cry in my love … I hold you against my own chest, against my own sacred heart. I comfort you. Where you're broken I bring health and healing. When people love each other they want the best for each other. I love you. I want the very best for you, and I can bring it about if you trust me. I can bring it about if you're open to a personal relationship that grows day by day. I want to give you more of myself every day. I want you to be still and listen. There is too much noise in the world. Shut off your TVs. Put away your newspapers for a day. Turn off your radio and listen, listen to the good news. Surround yourself with like-minded people for then I will be able to use you in ways that are far beyond your understanding. You will not even realize it. You won't even be aware of it till one day, one day when your life is ended on earth and you come home to me, you will see the fruit of your labor.

I am in the little things. Do not place your sights on the grandiose. Do not look for the spectacular. You see, I will bring about the spectacular as you walk with me, talk with me and listen to me and allow me to love you into wholeness, moment by moment, day by day, taking you from darkness to light more and more each day. You are children of the light and so I want you to shed your light onto those that I will bring into your life and show them the way to me, for in me their hopes, their dreams, will be realized with new eyes with a transformed mind and a heart on fire.

So trust me. Place yourself in my hands and trust that I love you enough that I will take care of all of your needs and I will place you exactly where you're supposed to be and I will go before you and prepare the way in which each of you are called to walk. I have brought you, each of you, here that you might hear my word, that you might feel my presence, that you might know that I am God and I love you.

9/8/16 (2 of 3)

My child, you're my little girl. I want you to crawl up when you feel lonely, confused or you're hurting. Crawl up on my lap. Allow me to embrace you. Allow me to infuse you with my love and my peace and my grace. You see, I'm calling you to a new thing. If you only knew how precious you are in my sight. I love the way your eyes sparkle. I love the way you're a little feisty. I love the way you laugh and it saddens me when you cry, even though you cry, often times, within. I know it all. But I want you to be open to a new deepening in our personal relationship. I want you to be open so that I might form you more fully into what I want you to be. You're my little girl. You always were and you always will be.

9/8/16   (3 of 3)

Much will change as you know it. But one thing that will never change is my love, my power, my divine will … that will never change. And yes, the deepest Southern regions … the South will become the North and the far most North will become the South and much will change. But my love is forever and always the same yesterday, today and forever. You, all you need to know is that I have my hand over each and every one of you. All you need to know is that I love each and every one of you and all who are mine will come to see the fulfillment of the great promises. You will see that it is true that I will never leave you nor forsake you, and though things will change, my love is unchanging, my power unchanging, my life unchanging. I am in all and over all. All I ask of you is to trust me and believe that I will never leave you. I will never forsake you and know that I work everything together for a greater good. Make no mistake about it, you will see these words come to pass. Keep your eyes on me and trust me and know that there's nothing to fear.

9/22/16

So many in this world, so many, say they can not see me, but are they looking for me? So many say they never hear me speak to them. But in the din of the world it's all the noise that comes at them from every direction

... the media, the noise in the world. Are they still? Do they listen to hear my voice? They feel that I am not close to them when in fact, I have not moved, **they have moved away.**

So many today cry out, they cry out for peace. They cry out for grace and help, but they feel there is no answer coming. I am the answer to every problem. I am the fulfillment of every hope and every dream and so they must come to understand that without me there's only moments of fleeting joy and for a time there is peace, for a time there is happiness, but happiness lasts for a moment or a day or a year. But when hope is placed in me, hope never disappoints. You see, even in the midst of sin, even in the midst of turning from me, turning from grace, I continue to call. Just as I called to Adam and Eve I continue to call to all those today who can not hear me, who can not see me, who can not sense my presence. They have eyes but they do not see and ears and they do not hear for I am with them always. And so I would have you speak to others of this great unconditional love for all else, all pleasure ... it's all fleeting. It will not last. Only my word will last forever and my word in their hearts will give them the kingdom. They have not realized that the kingdom of God is within them and so they feel empty. They do not realize that I dwell within them or they would not take me to the places they go. If they only knew how much I love them. If they only knew how much I cared. If they only knew how special and unique I made them ... nobody else like them, each one completely different, each one formed and fashioned in my heart before they were ever in their mother's womb.

So I ask you, will you go? Will you share my love, my mercy, my grace? Will you help them to understand that they have ears but do not hear me, eyes that fail to see me, and a heart that has grown cold. For I have a great gift for them. I will give them peace. I will give them the desires of their heart. You see, the very things they search for can not be obtained on their own. They must seek first the kingdom of God and all other things will be given unto them.

And so I leave you with this thought: all else will pass away, my word will never pass. There will be signs and wonders to see, but even then they will not believe until it's too late. And so now is the hour of mercy. Now is the hour of grace. Now is the hour to recognize my love working in you and through you. Oh, I want more for you and more for all those who do not know me than anyone could possibly imagine. Parents love their children and they have hopes and dreams of what they will grow into and all the ways that they will be a blessing to others. How much more with me? How much more does my heart rejoice when you are filled with a peace that nothing in the world could rob you of? How much more to feel the confident assurance that you can do all things because of me in you working through you? I have gifted you. I have blessed you with talent and skills and yet you fail to recognize often that I am the one who has given you these gifts and talents. Give them back to me. Offer them to me and watch me bless and anoint them and watch and listen and experience the power of my love entering your life and as I place this word in your heart and you share it with others, watch the power of my love at work in their lives.

So be ambassadors of my love, my unconditional love, my mercy. Go tell your story. Go share how I have moved in your life so that they might come to believe that I AM.

9/29/16

Have you not realized how often I have sent my mother? Have you not realized the urgency, not only in the amount of times that I have sent her to you, but the urgency of the message itself to fast and to pray. People look for an astounding bit of information that would come forth that would be different, it would be contrary, would be more dramatic, more earth-shattering. But you see, I send my mother to tell you the truth. I am the way, the truth and the life. This is the message that I ask her to bring in these urgent times. I send her time and time again. I send her all over the world to wake the world up, to speak a message of life and hope in a world of despair and death. I sent my mother into the world because she is the woman closest to my heart. I send my mother into the world to bring you this message of urgency, this message of victory, this message of love and mercy because she is mother of mercy for I am love and mercy itself.

So do not expect the spectacular to issue forth from her heart and lips. Instead, be attuned to the miraculous that says victory is ours, that tells you to fast and to pray and to live out the gospel message. This is why I send her that you would hear and obey. Fast, pray, and pray more.

10/6/16

Remember there will be many storms. Many storms will rage. And just like the Apostles who were in the midst of the storm ... they thought I abandoned them. They could not believe that I could sleep and they cried out to me, Lord don't you care? Don't you care that we're about to perish? What little faith they had even though I walked with them and talked with them and they saw miracles performed in their presence by my word, by stretching out my hand, and yet they did not think I loved them enough to save them. They did not realize that I am always in the midst of every storm, that I'm Lord over the winds and the seas. I'm Lord over the wind. I'm Lord over all the elements. And so when these storms come into your lives whether they're physical storms, emotional storms of heartache and grief, confusion and doubt, fear, despair ... they're real storms and I know that they affect you deeply.

But I say to you what I said to the apostles in the boat: I am with you. I am Lord over the storm, the storms that rage in the world, in your family, in your businesses ... I'm Lord over them. If you could just be at peace and realize that if I am with you who could be against you and that every single storm that rages against you, you grow stronger and stronger when you yield to my grace. I challenge you, yes. I stretch you, yes. I call you on, yes. I discipline you, yes, but I do all this because I love you. I do all this because I want you to believe and know without any inner doubt that whatever you see going on in the world, with every turmoil and circumstances that are trying to rob you of peace, remember this: in the midst of the storm I will place you in the eye of the hurricane. I will place you in the eye of the storm because in the very center of a hurricane is the most peaceful, calm place to be. And so the storms that rage around you and come against you and fill you with anxiety and doubt and fear … I am here. I am in the midst of all of it. You are my own. I will take care of you. Just because you can't see me doesn't mean I am not present. You don't see the sun on a cloudy, dreary, rainy day, but just as assuredly you know it exists, you know it's there. Can you not believe more in me and my presence than the weather? I mean what I say. My word is truth, the truth that can set you free.

So I say it again to you this hour, but it is for every moment of your life: guard your heart. Let this word sink into your heart and when the fears arise, when the storms arise and when you feel you're about to perish, that you can take no more, remember this: I am Lord over the storms. When you allow me to be Lord over your life you will be at peace like in the eye of a hurricane. I will keep you in a safe place. I will keep you in a place that you will be able to experience peace in the midst of the raging storms of life. I will never leave you nor will I ever. Regardless of the circumstances you are going through will I ever leave you or forsake you.

10/13/16

I call to you. I call to you by name. I call to speak to you directly. my word to you is "stand firm". Stand firm and allow not your heart to be troubled or your mind confused. I am a God of clarity. I am a God of love and all mercy, a God of love and mercy itself. And in these times, these times are filled with so much evil in the world … these times when the devil is running rampant seeking to devour those that he can. I tell you this: I am in you and with you … never give up. You see, when you are walking with me, my time is not your time, but my timing is perfect. It's perfect to work these things together for a greater good in your life.

Many times you feel I am not present. Many times you do not even think that I'm anywhere near you or that I could even hear you when you cry out to me, but I assure you, I am. I assure you that I am living in you and working through you and because the enemy is running rampant he will try to rob you of faith, of hope. He will try to deceive you, confuse you for sure. He will bring anger and bitterness and resentment forth. He'll put thoughts in your mind, but I tell you this: stand firm for I who am in you are far greater than he who is in the world. All he can do is tempt. He can put thoughts in your mind but he can not take thoughts out. He can entice you and lure you and deceive you, but it is only you who can make the decision to allow him in or to trust in me, your Lord and your God who reigns on high … who's Lord of your life … who helps you carry the cross … who heals your heart … who brings clarity of mind … who is the Prince of peace.

Do not be fooled. I say it again, do not be fooled and remember this: always and forever, light dispels darkness. I am the light of the world and you are mine, flesh of my flesh and bone of my bone. I shall watch over you. I shall lead you. I shall comfort you and I will take care of all of your needs. Remember the choice is yours. Who do you open your mind and your heart and your spirit to? All else is external. This decision is always internal, and I am within.

10/20/16

There's nothing to compare to my love. The greatest feeling you could experience with your senses ... it really can not even compare with my unconditional love for you. All the money in the world can not compare with the gift of my love which is priceless. All the gadgets, all the electronics, all the technology, all that you could have at your fingertips could never compare with my love, my power, my creativity, my wisdom and my knowledge. You see, they all come from me. I am the gift-giver. I am the promise-keeper. I say this to you that you might come to understand that all those pleasures that different things bring to you, to your senses, to your experience, to your lives ... nothing can compare with my love, for my love is everlasting from generation to generation. My love is constant, never ending, forever and always.

I have loved you with an everlasting love from the time I first conceived you in my own mind and fell in love with you with my own heart. Everything about you … the way you look, the way you walk, the way you talk, your mannerisms, your character, everything about you … it's from my creativity. I am the creator of all life. I am the creator of all things. All that is good comes from me so nothing can compare with my love. My love is extravagant. It's splendor in all its glory and yet you fail to recognize it throughout the day. I give you glimpses because you could not bear to be exposed fully. You would not be able to take it in. It is too sublime for you to handle and so I give you glimpses … a little surprise here and there. I send a special person into your life that knows you and loves you as you are. It's my love being manifested because nothing can compare with my love.

You see, it was you, the vision of you, that held me to the cross. It was for you that I stretched out my hands in obedience to my Father's will because I loved you. I love you at every moment and every instant of every day. I love you when you're broken and I come to meet you in the brokenness and I put those broken pieces back together to renew you and to restore you. I send refiners fire to refine you with the flame of my love, with the fire of mercy and power and grace. Nothing can compare to the love that I have for you. When I screamed out in excruciating pain: "Why have you abandoned me?" … you see, I was screaming for each and every one of you because I am outside of time and space and so in all your cries, forever and always, I answered: "Why have you abandoned me?" when I surrendered myself in obedience, when I laid down my life so that you would have eternal life.

I have loved you in your good days and your not-so-good days. I have seen the times that you have cried, cried because you felt you weren't appreciated and cried because you felt so hopeless at times. But you see, I have loved you and will always love you because I am love and mercy itself and the ocean of my mercy flows out from my heart to your hearts and the cry of my people. Nothing could compare with my love. And when you feel abandoned, when you feel rejected, when you feel that nobody understands you, when you feel that nobody's there to support you and hold you up when you want to drop, encourage you on when you want to give up, remember this night, remember these words: I cried out "Why have you abandoned me?" for all people, all time, and I answered it with my surrender when I offered up my life that you would one day be with me in paradise.

10/27/16

You know, I summoned you here tonight. Not only did I call you by name but I literally summoned you. I anointed the power, the power of my Holy Spirit to well up within you and bid you come to me. You see, I have so many plans in store for you, plans that you have not even yet conceived. And I call you here to affirm you, affirm you in my love, in my transforming power, and in the infinite depth of my mercy. I indeed have a plan for you. So often you look at others and see me at work in them and yet you fail to see me at work in you.

You see, my love is unchanging. No matter what you've done in the past, in the present or will do in the future, I will always love you. I wait for a heart that turns to repentance to come to me and then I will send you out, my child. I will send you out as wounded healers to bring my heart through your hearts to all those that I will bring you in contact with. These are tumultuous times make no mistake about it, but I remind you once again it is for a time such as this that I've called you and rallied my people. I'm waking up the Church. I'm shaking the very foundations and I call you, I call each of you by name, and I call you "friends", I call you "beloved", I call you "my brothers and sisters", I call you the "redeemed", I call you to march on, I call you to do the work that I've called you to do. You see, it is not for a few but for all of you who have been baptized in me, who have put me on.

Every one of you I have given gifts to. Oh, and I have loved you with an everlasting love. I've loved you in your brokenness. I've loved you in your sinfulness and I continue to call "Come, come back to me with all your heart" and you began to turn towards me and then I would give you a sense of my presence and you would receive an overwhelming sense of my presence within you. I want to make all things new. I want to heal and bind up wounds. I want to deliver all those who are bound through the chains of addictions. It will come to pass, I assure you. Do not give up.

Do not think I only choose those who use the gifts, those who walk in the path that I've called them. You see, I have called each of you and I've got a work for each of you to do but you have the freedom to say "yea" or "nay". Let your ears hear this word. Did I not choose twelve very imperfect men? Were not my other disciples also imperfect? Were many of them not broken? So do not loose heart for my arms are wide open to bring all my people to the wounded side of my heart. My arms and my heart are always open to all those who have been lost. Allow me to find you and I will protect you, watch over you. I will love you as no other one could .. completely and unconditionally.

I offer you the ultimate. I ask only that you would open your heart. I ask only that you would say "yes" and allow me to do the rest within you … to heal you, to set you free to be all that I call you to be, to transform you with my empowered grace, to transform you in my love and in my ocean of mercy. You see, I'm continuing to fill you with love and power and mercy. You have not arrived at the fullness of what I call you to be until one day you're home with me. You will know all and see all then. In the meantime I continue to perfect you. I'm like the refiner. I'm like the refinisher. The fire of my love burns away all impurities you know, and I am the refinisher that takes out and takes away the bruised wood, the cracks, the holes. I fill, I heal, I bind up … I love you.

11/10/16

There is no sin so great that my mercy can not wash away. I tell you to trust in my divine mercy. I tell you that I have loved you with a love that goes beyond all understanding. You see, I alone search hearts and souls. Even when you don't know why you did what you did, even though you wonder how you could even be capable of doing some of the things that you have done, I search the heart, I probe the soul and I know more than you yourself why you do the things you do. I want you to remember that when someone turns to me, when they turn with a repentant heart, oceans and oceans of my mercy flood that soul. They become whiter than snow and then I use them to go out and to touch others to bring the message of redemption, to bring the message of unconditional love. We look sometimes at a God who is all loving and all good and yet was I not myself nailed to a cross? But never forget it was love that kept me on that cross … love, my brothers and sisters, love … love for each and every one of you, love for all of my people. It's that love that kept me on the cross.

There will be trials and tribulations I assure you, but he who comes to destroy and kill … I come to renew and fill with grace. I am a God of mercy and love. You who are worried about your children let me just say this: as you stay faithful in prayer, as you turn to me in hope, my grace goes out to all of your children … grace upon grace upon grace. I am bringing them back. I am calling them from all over. Some have left The Church and entered other churches. Some have left The Church completely and no longer live a Christian life. Some people live in an altered lifestyle. But regardless of it all, am I not God? Is not everything in my control? Am I not the Lord of lords and the King of kings? I can deliver. I tell you every person who repents, if it's 10, 20, 30 times a day, I see their heart and in that repentance, as they turn to me, I flood their souls with grace. This is what is needed to bring you full healing and reconciliation. You are mine and I paid your price in full. I have redeemed. I have reconciled. I have made all things new.

Do not hold on to your sins from the past. When the devil whispers in your ear that you're a phony, when he whispers in your ear that you're not the Christian you think you are, that others think you are, know this: you are. Know this: when you are repentant you are as pure as the driven snow and I love you and that ought to be enough to know that I died for you and your sins so that I can redeem you and make you whole so that you could be a new creation in me and through me. Let your heart rejoice. Let the sun rise up in you and dispel the darkness. I am Lord over life itself. I am the alpha and the omega. I am the beginning and the end. I am the God who saves you.

12/1/16

Allow my light to shine brightly in you and through you. Allow my light to well up within you to dispel the darkness. You see, I call you and then I send you. I send you out to dispel the darkness to drive it away. So many people fear the dark and yet without even realizing it and recognizing the truth that they avail themselves and invite darkness in, and then they fall, they stumble in the dark. But you, I remind you that you have within you the light of the world and I call you to go out and bring that good news to a world that is in desperate need. I call you to be disciples of light. I call you to shine your light everywhere you go. A beam of light goes out and in the pitch dark of night when the light shines there is a clear pathway and the darkness is removed.

You are mine. You are my disciples. You are my apostles in this time, in this age, and so I send you out. I send you out to literally dispel the darkness. I ask each of you: Will you follow me? Will you follow me? Will you be a voice for those who have no voice? Will you be hope for those who have no hope? Will you bring my joy so that those who have no joy will experience joy to the full? I ask you, I do not impose my will on you. I impart it to you. I ask you to receive it, but again, I will not impose my will on you, but I do ask you to receive all that I have because I want to give it to each and everyone and I want to use you. I use you as a gift to be able to bring the light into the darkness, the light that shines, never ends, never dims, but continues to dispel and to drive out evil darkness.

I want you to think of what evil and darkness denotes: anger and resentment and bitterness, self-loathing, lack of confidence, hate, envy, lust … all those things are dark, to only name a few. Then I want you to think: who do you know that suffers in those ways? Who can you bring the light to? Think about it. That's what I call you to be, and blest are you who carry the good news, and blest are you who bring the light to drive away darkness and evil. If only they knew. There is no power, there is no power greater than my power, and the moment my light shines, the darkness is gone. So be bearers of light, and know this, that I'm beginning to move in new ways. Are you ready? Are you willing? Make no mistake about it, you are able when you yield to my power, the power of my Holy Spirit at work in you.

    You can not achieve grace no matter how hard you try. You can not make an effect on life for change. No matter how hard you try it won't last. It is only through grace. You can not achieve it on your own so I ask you to receive it and I will flood you with grace and light to be the bearers of good news in a world that's full of bad news, to be bearers of light, my light, to drive away darkness. Are you ready? Will you come along with me? Will you follow me and will you allow me to go before you and prepare the way. Remember, I do not impose, I propose to you. I do not impose my will but I ask you, as I impart it, that you would receive it.

12/8/16

    I want you to listen to my voice. I want you to be still and know that I am God in the midst of all the din, all the noise that takes place around you. Because as you learn to focus on me, on my word, on my life within you,

you become oblivious to all the noise in the world. I ask you always to remember who you are, that every son is a highly favored son, that every daughter is a highly favored daughter.

Regardless of what is going on in your lives, I ask you to do as my mother did, trust that my word would be fulfilled in you. And so I send you, I send you to be the good news. I send you to bring truth into a world that is full of lies. I send you to bring peace in a world that is in turmoil … and it will get worse. But I send you out that in the midst of the turmoil others will see a peace within you … the light they will be drawn to.

So I ask you to be still and to listen to my voice in the deepest part of your being, in the silence of your heart. I know there are many voices you hear. Some sound good. Some you begin to feel is the very answer to all that's going on in the world, but I tell you this: there is only one thing that will last. Everything else will pass away but my word. So I ask you to trust in my word. I ask you to read my word. Allow it to take root in your mind and in your heart and in your spirit. I ask you to take my word to others. I say this again: there are many miracles just waiting to happen but that my people would believe and trust that my word will be fulfilled.

I send you. I send you out to preach, to teach, to heal and deliver, particularly in your own families, not so much by your words but how you live the gospel message out so that others can look and see that you are authentic. There's many who speak a word, many who even perform miracles, what they call miracles. However, a day will come when I'll say I never knew them.

You, each of you … spend time with me. I have brought you here that you would feel my presence, that you would know without a doubt that you are loved, cared for, anointed, that I bring health and healing into your mind and into your bodies and spirit. Ask me for more. Ask me for more … more faith, more hope, more trust, more power. I will give it to you. I will trust you with my love, my mercy and my power. I ask you to be good stewards of the gifts that have been given to you. I ask you to pray for one another. I ask you to be the good news, and blest are the feet of those who carry the good news out into the world that is full of bad news.

Trust in me. Believe in me. Hope in me and you will see the power of the almighty at work, maybe not in the way that you expect power to react to circumstances, but a power that goes far beyond your understanding … a power that is above all powers, a might that is above all might, and at the same time the most tender, gentle heart of all hearts. It is this … this power, this love, this mercy that is the only hope.

12/22/16

See, I have found favor with you. I have blessed you in more ways than you could even possibly imagine. All the little ways that you see my hand at work in your life … they're little visitations, and it's because you are preparing your heart, because you are open. I am a God of power and might and all things are possible with me.

Even what man deems impossible, it is possible with me. These are the visitations where I come to each of you, and it's because you have humbled yourself, because you have prepared your heart, because you are looking for me for you are waiting for me. And so I say to you: you will not be deprived. I will bless you in many, many different ways. These will be my presents for you on my birthday.

You see, those who are filled with themselves, filled with pride and arrogance, those who set themselves above others, those who feel they're better than others … they've missed it. They missed my coming. Just as in the beginning, I did not come to those who were robed and wore beautiful clothing. I didn't come to the mighty, the proud, the arrogant. I didn't come to the kings and the queens of the day. I came in a little stable in Bethlehem and the first ones to really hear the good news were the little wise men, and before them the shepherds … the shepherds being the very first. You see, I came to them first because they were humble. They were always seeking my will, not their own. They were waiting in joyful hope for the messiah, hoping that I would come, not afraid that I would. And so I had the good news revealed to them first. That is why I reveal myself to you. When you are looking for me, when you are seeking me, when you are hungering and thirsting for me, it will not be in vain for I shall fill you with all good things. I will prosper you, not because you seek prosperity, but because I find favor with you. I will bless you with peace, the peace that the world wants but has no idea how to receive it, for I am the Prince of peace. I have come to reveal myself to you in the silence of your heart, in the very stillness of your being, and in the midst of the busyness of life I come and I will continue to reveal myself so that you might grow more and more aware of my life in you, and as you do, you will begin to decrease and I will increase within you.

The angels indeed sang to the shepherds: "Glory to God in the highest and peace to His people on earth". They weren't singing for me. They were actually singing for you so that all generations would know of the miracle of my love that took place in a little stable amidst the night and the cold and the foul odors. And so I say to you this night: when you look for me, you will find me. When you seek me, I will give you wisdom from above. I will give you joy where there is sadness. I will bring you peace where there is turmoil and I will bring you the miracle of my love.

I am never finished with you. I love you in spite of all the bad decisions you have made. I love you, and I love you into wholeness. You see, if it wasn't for your weaknesses you wouldn't need a savior. I came to save my people from their sins, and then when you receive that forgiveness, that salvation, that I stretch you and challenge you to go out and be bearers of the good news of the Gospel, and as you do, I will anoint you from head to toe and bless you. You will be cooperating with the power of my Holy Spirit at work in you and through you to bring the message of salvation while there is time. Get busy my people, get busy. This is indeed a time of mercy and grace. Go out to the highways and the byways and proclaim that Jesus Christ is Lord.

(END OF VOLUME IX)

Volume 10

Nihil Obstat
Rev. Msgr. Joseph G. Prior

Imprimatur
Archbishop Charles J. Chaput
Archiepiscopus Philadelphiensis
October 18, 2018

No portion of this book may be reproduced in any form without written permission from the Publisher:
Morning Star – New Dawn Ministries
P.O. Box 1446
Blue Bell, PA 19422
If unavailable in local bookstores, additional copies of this book may be purchased by writing to the Publisher at the above address.

Copyright, 2019 By Kathleen McCarthy
ALL RIGHTS RESERVED   ISBN 978-0-9641873-4-4

Artwork by Margaret M. Matt

1/5/17

I want you to take the fire of my love … I want you to take the fire and ignite a fire in the hearts of the people that you come in contact with. My fire … the fire that warms, radiates, warms and melts the coldest hearts, radiates warmth and brings a glow to the face, to the whole being of the person who carries my fire within them. That's you, you know. You carry the fire. This world is in need of the fire of my love. It needs to experience, once again, the warmth where hearts have grown so cold. It needs to experience again the purgation of being purged by this fire, the fire that doesn't harm but purges, purifies, cleanses, takes away the black, the darkness, until once again the hearts become pure. This fire … I have come to set a fire within you, but not for you alone. I come to set that fire upon the earth for all. This is indeed again a message of urgency. These are urgent times.

I am waking up the Church. I have even shaken the deepest foundations and my cry is "WAKE UP!" Wake up and realize your deliverance is at hand. Wake up and realize that you have a mission, that you have a purpose. The purpose is to fulfill my plan on the earth. Think of it. You carry fire within … the fire of my Spirit. It is this fire that is contagious. It is this fire that will draw others to you. They will see the fire of my love within you. They will feel the radiant heat beginning to well up within them as you ignite that fire with just even a spark of my love.

Now is the hour and now is the time to go therefore and make disciples, to go therefore and proclaim the truth, to go therefore and make friends of enemies, to go therefore and give a word of truth to set others free who are hell bound. Make no mistake about it, this is why I am sending you out. I'm sending you out that others might not be lost. I have called you and I have placed you in the midst of my fire and I call you to fan it daily. Fan the fire of my love that it will not grow dim within you. Seize the moment. I breathe my breath upon you ... my *"Ruah"*, and I breathe my breath into you that you might take the fire of my love and the breath of my Spirit to those who are in need, who do not realize that there is nothing that can separate them from my love except for their own free will.

Now is the hour. Now is the time. Remember, you carry the fire within. Go light a fire wherever you go, the fire of my love that will warm them, and at the same time as they draw close to the warmth, they will be renewed with new life through the breath of my Spirit and they shall become whiter than snow.

1/12/17

There are many battles, many battles indeed that are going on in the world, but I want you to know that all the battles that you wade into for my name and for my glory that you are victorious, not a victim. I want you to remember always and never forget that in each one of my warriors I send you into battle because <u>you</u> are the strongest. Often times you forget that I who am in you and working through you is far greater than he who is in the world. I ask you and remind you again to put on the armor of God for you are in a battle, a battle for souls, because you yield to the power of my Spirit in you, longing that no souls would be lost, and so you cooperate with my grace.

But again I say, do not moan and groan and complain about why everything happens to you, about why all these things go wrong in your life, about why many are sick among you. The battle goes to those who are battle-worthy, to those who are the strongest, and the reason is because the enemy comes and he comes to rip down, destroy, devour. He comes to bring confusion and doubt. He comes to pit one against the other. He comes to divide. But you, you are called to bring the healing balm from Gilead. You come with the power of my Spirit at work in you. You are more than a conqueror because I am in you and working through you. Do not look at yourselves as victims. That's what those who have no belief in the power of the almighty do, but keep your eyes on me. Remember that I dwell within you ... the living God ... God of the living. So I say to you, never forget, never ever forget that I will fight in you and through you. You are not alone and consider yourself blessed to carry the cross because it is through the cross that I have redeemed you and in the cross there is power.

So do not complain. Do not moan and groan and gripe. Instead, consider yourself blessed to be my warriors. Consider yourself blessed that I find you battle-worthy and ready. So go therefore, go therefore and proclaim the God of power and might and the God of mercy and love.

1/26/17

So many people do not realize, do not even give it a second thought, that they have the "Great Pearl", that they have the greatest gift they could ever have: "The Pearl of Great Price", and yet they don't want it. They don't want to be blessed by it. Instead, they search and seek after the pearls in the world. They try to seek after riches, after all the pleasures. Even though they're fleeting, they seek after all the pleasures. They seek after all the things in the world that will bring them to ruin and their moments of peace or happiness are all temporary ... so temporary. And yet when they continue to search after these things and to seek them out, not realizing they had "The Great Pearl of Great Price", they wonder why they're unhappy. They wonder why nothing fulfills them. They'll go after relationship after relationship after relationship seeking it in a person. They seek to climb the ladder to be the most popular, the most famous, the one that everybody gives accolades to, to be the best of this and to be the best at that. And yet inside, they find when they get to the top of the ladder, they're still empty. You see, they do not understand or comprehend in any way at all that what I give them: my word, my life, my love, is worth more than any of the goods in the world all put together, all the money in the world all over the world all put together, all the greatest relationships in the world all put together. None of it can compare with my love. With "The Pearl of Great Price" nothing can compare. And so they throw it away or they pawn it off or they put it aside thinking one day they'll come back to their faith, one day when I have achieved all that I want to achieve in the world. They think one day they'll turn to me when they have received the riches of the world and the pleasures of the world. What they do not understand is they might never have that day and so their souls are in jeopardy day after day.

      I call to them all the day. I visit them in many different ways throughout the day. I work in situations and circumstances and when those situations and circumstances happen, they curse me not realizing again "The Pearl of Great Price", that I'm intervening in their lives trying to draw them close to the truth that "I AM". These are hearts that have grown cold. These are eyes that are closed and refuse to see. These are ears who do not hear. These are those who I continue to love. These are those that I continue to send people into their lives time and time again to bring the good news. But again, they remain closed always seeking something more in their mind, something better. Fools they are for sure for they know not when the hour comes when I will call them to give an accounting of their life.

      You see, I call each of you to be a contradiction to the world. I call each of you to bring peace where there is hate. I call each of you to fill those moments in time when there are such gaps and lack of love in society. I call you to love. When no one else will love, I ask you to love. When you don't feel like forgiving when you've been hurt or wounded, I call you to continue to forgive. When you feel that you've given of yourself, of your time, of your talent, of your money, and to you, you see it goes to no avail ... continue to give of your time, of your talent, of your money, for you see, my ways are not your ways. But as you walk in the fullness of my truth and you live according to my word, being a contradiction in the world, sowing love where there's hate, forgiveness in times of cruelty and abuse, you will have chosen the better part. You will be the ones who have continued to carry the light into the darkness. It is you who carry my word within you. You are my tabernacles. You see, you carry my presence within you and because you do that's a responsibility, a responsibility to reach out when you don't want to ... reach out anyway. When you don't want to forgive, forgive anyway. When you don't want to speak up for fear of rejection, speak up anyway. You see, I am working through your words, through your actions, through your silence. Continue to walk according to my word. You see, for all, your only hope is in me. I am your hope and when you believe in me and walk and live and move in me, you will find a peace and a joy and a happiness when you know that you are truly blessed because I live in you. I work in you and love you into wholeness day by day. I ask you to go and be a contradiction to the world. You see, that's what the world really needs. The world really needs a demonstration of unconditional love.

2/2/17

I know so many times that you do not understand my ways. My ways are not your ways, but I have told you this in the beginning so that when things come into your life, when crosses are heavy and trials are many, instead of seeing darkness I want you to realize that, you see, I am Lord over all. I'm Lord of all life. I'm the first and the last. I'm the beginning and the end. For all those who have suffered, I have suffered too with you. I have given you the grace to give me your burden and allow me to take it into my own heart and with the light of my love to send it back into your life with grace and light to dispel the darkness that it had left. I am the very reason for your hope. I am love and mercy itself. My mother is indeed the mother of mercy, the mother who carried me in her womb, and as my mother, was not her heart pierced and torn as well as mine when she saw me suffer. She knew that I was being taken from her, yet she knew without a doubt that if I gave her her Son I would surely give Him back again.

    I would have you know, and I would not have you doubt this: I AM. I am Lord over all. I give and I take away, and one day when you realize that my ways are the best ways, you too will cry from your heart: "Blessed be the name of the Lord". It is only by my name that everyone on the earth, <u>everyone</u> on the earth, can only be saved by my name. The enemy knows the power of my name and they tremble. I ask you to be assured that my name is above every name and that I am working in and through every situation in your life. I want to put peace in your heart where there's heartache and trials, where there's grief and sorrow, where there's confusion and doubt, where there's fear and anxiety. If I loved you enough to die for you, to lay down my life that you might have life, can you not trust me with your life and the lives of all those that I have placed in your life? I am the author of all life.

I tell you that your loved ones are closer to you than you could have ever possibly conjured up or imagined in your mind. They see you. They pray for you that you too might be with them where they are, because they are with me. I want you to know that whatever cross you bear, I will give you the grace to bear it. I want you to know that with every tear you have ever shed, I will fill you with a peace and yes, a joy, a joy that goes beyond all understanding because it will be my joy. I want to put a new song in your heart. I want to touch your mind and renew it and heal it. I want to wash away your tears, comfort your soul, because I love you. I want you to see my love in the people that I place in your life. I want you to come to know that I am your liberator. I want you to know and trust me that although my ways are not your ways, you can not see the future. You can not see what has taken place in the past, but for me, it is always "now". I see all and I know all and I want you to trust me as my mother trusted my Father to know that one day I would return to her, that I would rise from the dead to show her the fulfillment of the promise that I am the resurrection and the life.

     I do not want you to beat yourself up for the past because I am the liberator. I have come to heal your heart and set you free, to renew and restore your dignity. I want to heal your mind, your heart and your spirit. I want others to see you and when they see you I want them to see my word alive and working in you and through you so that they will know that I died for all and I am in all.

3/2/17

There's a great rebellion, a rebellion that is rumbling, growing all over the world. I would have you know there will be many, many who will speak and they say their words are from me, but they will not be from me. They will be from the Deceiver. Many people will panic. Many people will fear. Many people will join the rebellion, this rebellion that is rumbling, rising up.

But I say to you, for you who believe, for you who are my children, flesh of my flesh, bone of my bone, for you, you will be bright lights shining in the darkness. You will draw others. You will save them through the power of my love and my Spirit at work in you by standing firm, by being a light shining brightly in the darkness. I tell you there is much work to be done. Do not be deceived. Do not look here and there. Do not let your heart be troubled nor let your mind be confused or deceived. I speak. I lead. I guide, and my word will be a lamp unto your feet. Be not deceived. Many false prophets will rise up among you, but I tell you this, have ears to hear this and the wisdom to absorb it: I do not contradict myself. I say it again: I do not contradict myself.

The Church, my Church, the one I instituted myself, has a rich deposit of faith handed down right from my own apostles. You are my apostles in this day. Do not be led astray. Do not have your ears tickled and do not let fear strike your heart. They are tactics from the enemy to deter you from walking, walking on the journey that I have called you to: being a light to dispel the darkness. The enemy trembles and trembles with fear for you, you are my light in the darkness. Allow my light to shine brightly. Do not fear but be filled with courage and holy boldness for the time has come when you are called, anointed, blessed and sent with the authority that was given to the Church, empowered to bring truth, not a watered down truth, but the truth that mother Church holds close to her bosom. Many will leave. There will be a great apostasy like nothing that has been seen before. But you, you stand in the truth. Remain in the truth and know this: I will never abandon you. I will never leave you nor forsake you. Trust in me. Trust in my love, my mercy and my power. You shall be "Overcomers". Trust, trust in my mercy and my love.

3/16/17

I see you, each and every one of you. I see you with your efforts, with the desires of your heart to walk this Lenten Journey, to take the road that leads to the cross ... my cross. I tell you this night for all who have come to experience my love and my mercy, my power and my grace ... you know that your prayers, your sacrifices, the desire of your heart to please me ... they all rise up like incense. Time and time again I have shared with you that to embrace the cross brings power, for in your weakness my power is at its greatest work and depth in you and through you.

I gave a charge. I charged you with preaching the Gospel when it was convenient, yes, but even when it was inconvenient ... through trials and tribulations, through suffering and grief, through the joys and triumphs and all the wonderful days. Preach, teach ... this is what I've commanded you to do, and you are doing it. Make no mistake about it, I know how difficult it is to walk with the weight of the cross. Did I not fall three times, but I did not stay down. It was my love that drove me to get up again. It was an obedience to the call. Yes, obedience even to the cross unto death. As I often say to you: I did it for you, for each and every one of you, for all those who have gone before you, all those that are present, and all those who are still far off. I did it for each and every one.

I want you to know that I see your struggles. I see your pain and your sorrows and your grief and I capture, as I've told you many times, every tear that you shed, and one day you will see as I capture those tears I pour them out, full of grace, into the lives of others who have no one to pray for them. So every time you embrace the cross, every time you suffer, every time you grieve, every time, in joy and thanksgiving, you offer me praise and glory and honor, all of these things I take them and I receive them as you offer them to me, and I pour out grace upon grace upon those that you have prayed for, those in your household, in your family, in your neighborhoods, your parish, your friends, and yes, even your enemies. I pour out amazing grace through every single act of love you offer to me.

So I tell you, continue on the journey. I tell you the key, the answer to every stress, to each anxiety and fear, to all those who feel that they can not go on, that the road is too hard, I send this grace. Many times I send my mother to pour out the grace that is needed for all those who love her, for all those who know that I have given her to you ... my mother ... your mother ... our mother. And so I say, rejoice and be glad. I say to you, count it all as grace and blessing and I ask you to continue on this journey. Offer everything to me in love. I remind you of who you are, of who you belong to. I tell you, you too are most highly favored daughters, you too are most highly favored sons, and everyone, everyone ... male, female, young and old ... each one has been given the charge to preach the Gospel. So go out and share the good news in the midst of all the bad news in the world. Smile at others, especially those who have lost hope and are depressed. Reach out to those who are hurting, broken, wounded, on their way to Gehenna and the lost. Reach out, and every act of kindness and love and compassion, I will bestow back on you a hundredfold. They must see me in you, and when they do, the light will shine brightly to dispel the darkness in their lives.

So go, therefore, and make disciples in the name of the Father and of the Son and of the Holy Spirit.

3/23/17

Is it not good to be still, and to know that "I AM", that I am your God and you are my people? Often times, and more often than not, you wonder: Lord, I long to hear your voice. Lord, where are you? Lord, I cry out to you, please answer me. And yet, you fill your mind and your heart and your lives with so much noise. You fill your heart and your mind and your spirit and your lives with all the ways that *you* feel that God will answer you. You fill your lives and minds and hearts and spirits with the things of the world thinking you can find me there and you will know "my way" from the things in the world, yes, even those things that are good. They too can be abused. They too can be used to draw you away from me rather than allow you to cling to me. Many times you'll wonder why these thorns are in your side. Many times you'll ask that they be removed. Some are physical thorns. Some are emotional thorns. Some are spiritual thorns. You wonder why you are not receiving the grace, why you are not receiving the voice to lead you, to heal you, to guide you, but it's because you are not still. I can not speak to the silence of your heart if you do not allow me <u>into</u> your heart.

  Why is there sickness? Why is there heartache and why do you find life burdensome at times? Why do tragedies take place? When will you heal me, Lord? When will you free me, Lord? When will you speak to my heart, Lord? These are some of the many petitions that come to me. Many times there's redemptive suffering and often times people beg that that suffering would be removed. Again, sometimes it's physical suffering, often times, emotional suffering, and most times, spiritual suffering. But you see, many times, particularly in redemptive suffering, the suffering can be used as *"eye openers."* Many need to have their eyes opened so that they can see more clearly, come to love me more fully, walk with me with purpose and focus.

So I ask you to trust me. I ask you in the midst of all the things that are going on in your lives, in your country, in your families, in your businesses ... I ask you to trust me. Am I not the All-Knowing, All-Seeing? Am I not the Infinite One? Does not everyone have their being because of my word and my will? And so you need to take the quiet time. You need to come away with me to be still and trust when you feel that your prayers are not being heard, when you feel your prayers are not being answered, when you feel like you have been forgotten or abandoned. I assure you quite the contrary is taking place. Many things, many circumstances, many trials and tribulations ... I will use these very things that you do not understand as *"eye openers"* for those who have eyes but can not see and ears and can not hear and who have a heart that has not been opened to me.

So I ask that you trust me. I ask you to thank me for all that you have, for all and everything that is good is from me from above and, yes, even those things you do not understand, even those things that you ask me to take away from you, to remove the thorns ... thorns of drinking, alcohol abuse has ruined many a life and many a family, drug abuse the same, promiscuity, pornography ... I could go on and on. These things not only rob you of peace and dignity and grace and strength and hope, but they rob you from feeling the power of my work in you and through you.

Do not let the enemy spread his lies and deception. Know this: I alone am the way and the truth and the life. Never forget, where there is no way I will make a way and that I always work everything to good even when you can't see it, feel it. Trust ... place your hope and your trust in my divine love and mercy, not only for you and your household, but for your families, friends, and all those that you are praying for. Trust me. I see all, I know all and I work all together for a greater good for those who love me.

3/30/17

I want to remind you, each of you who suffer persecution, you who feel misunderstood and often times ridiculed and rejected, the times when you feel frustrated, the times when you feel does anybody really understand what's going on in the world today, that there is indeed a dimension of darkness that is trying to come against the light and, in these days and at this hour, evil is raising its ugly head in every place and everywhere.

But I remind you that I am the light of the world. I remind you that light always dispels the dark. Even the tiniest light gives a path … a path of light and the darkness in gone. Do not fear the darkness. I say to you that you, you must shine your light brightly. You must do spiritual combat. You walk not alone for I accompany you on the way. I send a bastion of angels to surround you. I give you my own armor to put on you. I told you before that you are battle-worthy, you just do not realize it. I tell you now that you must rise, rise up and be my light. You must speak to others who are walking in darkness. Do not be afraid of the dark for you are children of the light. You must share the truth with those who are in darkness. You must tell them of my great love and my mercy.

Yes, you too will be rejected by those that hear you. You too will be ridiculed. You too will be talked about and no one could blame you in the world if you remain silent, but the world, I remind you, is passing away and I tell you now that light and darkness will clash in such a way that there will be cataclysmic things that will happen. I say this to prepare you, not to frighten you, and I ask that you would not look at the things that are going on in the world but that you would look to me, your Redeemer, your Savior. I have a plan and my plan comes from my heart to the heart of my people. My heart is a "safe refuge" and unless they know the truth that when they turn away from their evil ways that they will never die, that I will love them into wholeness and that I'm a tender, loving and merciful God. When they hear this truth from your lips who have experienced my infinite love and mercy, my tenderness and my power, when you talk about "you" and not "them", when you point your finger to your heart, not at them, when you share your story and the power of my Spirit that has moved in you and through you, then they will come out of the darkness into my glorious light.

So I say to you, for all those in your life who you feel have walked away, turned away, and for those who have never ever walked away, I send you as a messenger. I send you empowered and I send you with fire within, and when that fire comes forth, my fire within each and every one of you, it will do my work. The fire of my word, the fire of my Spirit will bind up wounds, will heal physically and spiritually and emotionally. It'll bring pardon and peace and grace and strength and, oh, so much more.

So arise. Do not slumber but be alert for the enemy is on the prowl. But you, you are victorious for you believe that I am the resurrection and the life. Speak under the influence of my Holy Spirit so it will not be your words that others hear but my words coming forth from you. It'll be my love and my power that others will experience as I move in you and through you to touch the hearts that have grown cold, to touch the ears and open those who have refused to hear the truth before, and to open the eyes of those who refuse to see the truth that would set them free.

You are my hands and my feet and my voice. Bring me present to my people. Focus only on me. Focus on the mission that each of you have from your baptism.

4/20/17

Do you know that I walk and enter your journey, the journey of your life? I walk and enter in to conversation, to prayer. I enter into the silence. I enter into your heart, to your mind, to your spirit, and I speak from my heart to your heart. You see, I have anointed you. I have called you by name and I have allowed you to be baptized into my own death so that you might live with me. I give you new life and it happens throughout the day, throughout the weeks, throughout the years, throughout the journey of your life. I enter in to your conversation, your prayers. I enter into your thoughts, and when I do, my light will begin to have the darkness fade, the darkness of your doubts, your fears ... yes, your anxieties that you suffer much with.

     I am with you. Many times you do not recognize me. Do you too need to see to believe? Do you too have to see before you go and be my witnesses? *(This Sunday's Gospel was about Thomas not believing unless he saw for himself).* I don't want you to know about me. I don't want you only to read about me. I want you to <u>know</u> me ... to know me: true man and true God ... Father ... the Father who created you while you were in your own mother's womb. I fashioned you while you were still in secret being formed and then I called you forth and gave you life. I breathed my breath into you ... that *"Ruah"*, the breath of my Spirit so that you would be my witnesses. And so I want you to be evermore aware of recognizing me throughout your day. I want you to recognize me in one another. I want you to recognize me even in the most difficult set of circumstances because I want you to believe in my promise: I will never leave you nor forsake you.

     Though you have eyes and do not see me, believe that I am here, for I am. You speak of me, but do you know me? You see, I want to reveal myself more and more, day in, day out, moment to moment. I want to deliver, I want to deliver you from any influence of the evil one. I want you to be sober. I want you to be at peace. I do not want your heart to be troubled. I do not want you anxious, and so I walk with you. You're not even aware that I am. I see your tears when they drop and as I have told you, I capture every tear you ever shed. And when your heart is broken, sometimes even crushed in times of grieving, in times of sorrow, remorse, repentance, brokenness … in these times I am with you. I want you to turn to me. I want you to turn to me and seek my mercy, my unfathomable mercy. This is the gift, the gift that I give to you … my mercy. You see, did I not die for the sinners? While you were still sinners I laid down my life and died for each and every one, every one of you. In your disobedience my obedience led me to the cross. I paid the price for each and every one for all the sins that you will commit, for all the failings that you will have, for all the doubts, all the fears.

I ask only that you hope in me. I ask that you trust in me, trust in my promise. Never forget that throughout the day I walk with you. I live through you and I love you unconditionally. Continue to follow me. Continue to seek me, for when you call me I will come. When you seek me, you will find me. You wait too long and that's why anxiety and fear set in. I want you to grow in love with me so much that you will trust that whatever is happening in your life that I am Lord over it all just as I am Lord over all the elements. I'm Lord. I'm the creator of all. Do not, again I say, do not fear. Be not dismayed. Do not loose hope. You see, my plan is being carried out and I want you to be my witnesses for others will read your story, others will read your story and be brought out of the darkness into the light.

5/4/17

    I have called you. I've beckoned to you because I want to ignite a fire in your heart. I want to enlighten your mind and your heart and your understanding of the depth of my love for you. I want to ignite a fire within, a fire that burns so brightly that others will be drawn through the warmth of my love at work in you flowing out to them. There is no such thing as coincidence. I've called you by name and you have come because I have beckoned to you. I've drawn you here tonight. Know this: I know the fire has grown dim but I want you to know that the fire that has grown dim will not be quenched. The fire will be fanned in the breath of my Spirit and the fanning of the flame will well up mightily within you.

    I call you to listen, listen to my word. My word is transforming. My word severs everything in you that is not of me and then the fire of my Spirit seals my love and my power at work in you. You have not felt that fire in some time. My love is not a "feeling". I did not feel the fire on the cross but I did believe, in my humanity, the Father's word that He would call all of you, that He would call to all humanity that they would come to know me, to love me, and to serve me. The Father has loved each and everyone of you and He beckons you to stand in the gap for one another. He beckons you for all those in your family who are hurting, wounded, broken, all those that are suffering, those who are living a lifestyle that's contrary to my word, all those who have wandered off, all those who are living in sin and debauchery, all those who are trying to fill those empty places within their heart and their soul trying to heal the pain, the suffering.

Never doubt that I have called you here. Never doubt that I hear the cry of the poor, not the cry of the poor that you're thinking of when I say these words to you, meaning those who are in such financial need. Of course, the poor you always have with you and I want you to share what you have with them, but I talk of the poor in spirit. That's what I call each of you to be: poor in spirit ... to depend on me and to stand in the gap to pray for those who wander off, who curse me, who mock me, who mock you because of me. I want you to stand in the gap and pray for one another. I want you to never forget those who do not know me. Those who say they do not believe in God will one day come to believe in me, one day will come to know me, because they have known you. I call you and I call you by name. I tell you to come and follow me.

I wonder if you realize the gift you have been in others lives? I wonder if you realize the prayers that I have answered for you as you have cried out to me time and time again? I wonder if you realize just how much I love you? I'm your father and I want to love you into wholeness and through you I want to love others into wholeness because of you. Stand in the gap for one another. I hear your cry and I am answering your prayers and I am working in the midst of your confusion and your doubt and your anxiety. You see, I know all things, you don't, and so you worry, you get anxious, you fear. Trust in me and I will work everything, and I mean "everything", for good because you love me.

5/18/17

Are you worried about your children? Do you come with a troubled heart? Are you worried about your business? Are you worried about the situations that you find yourself in and you don't know how to get out of? Are you worried about the past and does it hold you captive? Are you concerned about the future ... what is taking place in the world ... what's happening in the government ... what's happening in the financial side of the world? Are you worried about the economy of your own business, your own life, loved ones?

These are things that you must entrust into my care. I am the one who holds all things under my domain. Nothing happens without me allowing it for a purpose and a plan. I am putting things in place. I'm putting them in place so that when I move others will say it is The Lord. I don't want you to be concerned, I don't want you to doubt. I don't want you to be filled with anxiety and fear and worry about your children or mates. They were mine first. I loved them first. I breathed my life into them. Do you think for one moment that I love them any less than I love you? Do you think for one moment I will not continue to call out to them, call their name and draw them to me? Do you think I will not distribute grace, the grace that is needed for them to come and follow me? Are you so "puffed up" that you think it depends on you, that you think it depends on the circumstances in life? No.

I call you to trust. I am the Lord your God who heals you. I am the Lord your God who sets you free. I am the Lord your God who breathed life into you and all of humanity. You get a headache thinking about all that falls on your shoulders ... you worry, you fear, you doubt, you have anxiety. I've said this to you before: all that worry, anxiety and fear can not change tomorrow, but it certainly will rob you of the peace that I give you today. Give me your worries. Place your worries in my heart, your fears and your anxieties. Do you not think I am bigger than all your problems? Do you not think I am more powerful to fulfill my promises? Come, come and follow me and give me your burdens so that I can set you free. I am about to do a mighty work and I want you to be open, open to the plans I have ... the plans for you, the plans for your children, the plans for your families and a plan for your business.

I am the Lord your God who heals you. I am your healer. I love it when you acknowledge that. I love when you sing praise, songs of worship. I love when you turn your heart and mind and spirit to me in honor and glory. Why? *For you*, because it brings peace and grace and strength and courage and hope *to you*. Come to me with all your concerns and your fears and your doubts. Be a warrior. Be my warriors. Trust in my power at work in you and through you, and trust your family to me, trust your children, your businesses and your life. Place your hope and trust in me, that's when you become "free", that's when you experience my joy, my joy which will be complete in you. Trust me, and trust me more, and trust me again, and more still. I am the way, there is no other. Come and follow me. I have a plan, a purpose and I will reveal it. Trust me. Again, trust me even more.

5/25/17

I am love and mercy itself. I am indeed the alpha and the omega, the first and the last. I am your Lord and your God and there is no other. I want you to know, I want you to begin to understand the great cost, the cost of laying down my life for your life, the cost of being betrayed, broken, wounded, alienated, rejected, blasphemed against, having my flesh torn away from my body. How could this happen? How can this happen ... truly God and truly man? How could it have happened? It happened because I love you, I have always loved you. I love you when you think I don't hear your prayers. I love you when you walked away from me. I love you when you came back to me. I have always loved you. I want to lay my healing hands upon you. I want to renew you in mind and body and spirit. I want to wash away your tears. I want to comfort your soul. I want to renew your hope and your faith and your trust in me. I want you to begin to understand that although you have been loved, no one could ever love you like I love you. I have loved you from the moment I conceived you in my own mind. I have loved you from the time I fashioned and formed you in secret in your mother's womb. I loved you the first time that you came forth and were born into the world, and I breathed my breath into you to give you life. You see, I've always loved you. There's nothing you could have ever done or ever will do that would make me love you any less.

When my heart was pierced, it was pierced for you. Think of it ... pierced for you! When my soul was grieving, even unto death, I was grieving for you. Allow me to bring you a little deeper into my love, allow me to inebriate you in my body and my blood. Will you allow me to be Lord over your life? Allow me to serve you. Me serve you, yes! I assure you I can do a much better job with your life than you could ever possibly imagine doing yourself. Oh, I see you try. I see you try to make your own way. I see you try to do the things that you think should be done and you think you know the way that they should be done. I wait and yet you do not ask. I wait and you do not ask me for wisdom, knowledge, discernment, prudence. How long have you heard me say through the years: "Turn to me all of you who are heavily burdened and I will give you rest." I ask you now to place your life fully and completely into my hands, and I know that you can only do it sometimes moment by moment. That's all I ask is "now." Love me "now." Trust me "now." Give me your problems and struggles, your hurts, your wounds, your broken heart, your crushed spirit … give it to me "now." I will not "take" but I will "receive."

  Give me your children, the children that you feel have wandered away, the children that you feel have lost their way, the children you feel have no faith. I assure you, I am the one, I am the only one, there is no other who can breathe new life into them. I assure you that I am the only one who can forgive you and forgive others that you have been unable to forgive for the hurts, the rejection, the betrayal. I can forgive them in you and through you. Give them to me. I want to give you new life. I want to give you my joy. I want to lift your heart and your mind and your spirit. I want you to call to me.

I want you to come to me, but I will never force you. I want you to remember that I did it all for you.

It is said in the scriptures: "A suffering servant." I suffered greatly, my people, in my humanity. I hurt so much I could not even think straight. My pain racked my body from head to toe. But I surrendered all to my Father. I ask you to do the same and allow me to take your burdens. I died for them, why should you hold on to them? Offer them to me and in their place I will give you grace and peace, strength, courage, hope, and I will give you back the joy of your salvation.

6/1/17

Do you realize that I call each and every one of you by name? Do you realize that I draw you together, my own children, flesh of my flesh and bone of my bone, to pour out my gifts, my love, the anointing and power of my Spirit, on you, so that you then can be anointed to go forth and bring the power of my Spirit and the gifts of my Spirit to others, to fan the flame, not only in your own hearts, but in the hearts of those that you will come in contact with? Do you realize that I call you here to nourish you, to feed you, to teach you, to speak to your hearts? When you leave do you bring me with you? Do you ponder my words? Do you allow my words to touch your heart, to comfort your soul, to encourage you on your way?

I speak to each and every one of you. I want you to have the wisdom to know that I call each one of you to a work. I call each of you to mission, to join in with the mission of Holy Mother Church. You see, it was from the cross that I redeemed you, that I began this one, holy, catholic and apostolic Church and it was from the Church that I called you forth from being a pagan to being a child of God ... my child. I want you to remember that I call you to stay together and fellowship. I call you together to love one another as I have loved you as the Father has loved me. Can you imagine that? Can you really understand and comprehend in a deep way that as the Father has loved me so I love you? You see, I love you, I love you with all my heart and soul. When I walked the earth before you were even born, I went to redeem you before you even came into being. That is why I instituted my Church, that is why I instituted the sacraments so that I could continue to feed you and nourish you and that through the infusion of my Spirit in you working through you that you would begin to understand more fully the life I have called you to. I have called you to speak when everyone else is quiet. Even if you stand alone, I call you to speak the truth, but always in love. I call you to go out and bring the message, the good news, that the desire of my heart is that we would be one, you and me, me and you, and that we would be one in the Father.

    I want you to take your baptism seriously. Do any of you know the date you were baptized? I bet you'll never forget your birthday. I bet you'll never forget the day you graduated. You'll never forget your wedding day. Many of you will not forget the date of your Holy Communion or your Confirmation, but very few, but I bet very few of you remember this most important day when you were baptized ... the day you were given new life, the day I called you mine, the day I called you to be in the world and not of the world.

Use your gifts, my people. Don't let them lie dormant within you. I have given you much. I want you to find out the day you were baptized. Let me say this again: I want you to find out the date that you received new life through being baptized, when you died and rose again through me, through new life, when you became mine for I have a plan for you and it's important that you know your roots. It's important that you know that I called you out of the world and separated you from the world so that you could go back into the world and bring them truth. The day I called you into new life, into being part of my mystical Body, that day should be a day that goes down in your heart and mind and spirit as a day of new life for you. The more you grow in the awareness of that new life that was infused into you, the more powerful of an instrument you will be. I am the divine physician and I myself will use the tools that I have given you and I will work in you and through you with those tools to build up the kingdom of God. Ponder that. Ponder when I gave you new life, when I set you free, when you became a child of the living God.

6/22/17

There are so many stiff-necked people, so many that have ears, eyes, minds and hearts closed. Many times I prompt you. I prompt you to reach out to those who's eyes, minds, hearts, ears seem to be closed. Many times it's children, your own children. Many times it's your mate. Many times it's people that you love ... your siblings, your good friends, your acquaintances. I would not have you be afraid, do not be afraid to speak truth. It doesn't depend on you, but I ask you to rely on me working through you. You see, it's my truth. My truth sets free. It sets free those that are bound. I ask you to put away your fear and your anxiety of what others will think of you. Believe me, it's more important what I think of you.

You see, I have faith in you. Many times when you see that prayers aren't answered, or you feel that they're not, I assure you it's because I know you have what it takes to work through it, and so you see, I'm giving you the grace to do just that. I am moving in you and through you. I am answering your prayers and the prayers of all those who call upon me. I don't want you to be fearful or anxious. I don't want you to be afraid, ever, to speak the truth because when you do you miss an opportunity to set someone free ... to plant a seed of faith, to plant a word of hope, to nurture forgiveness, to enlighten one's mind, one's heart, one's spirit. You think it depends on you so you don't speak out. You're silent even though you know the truth that you've been set free by, but you don't want to be embarrassed, uncomfortable or looked at as one who is a religious fanatic. It's not about religion, it's about faith, hope, trust.

Again I say to you, look at me as your example. You're my followers. How many people betrayed me? How many people ignored me, rejected me? How many people left me because they could not accept the truth? So can you expect anything different if you follow me? But you see, I paid the price in full for your children, your mates, your friends, your acquaintances and even those who you struggle with, those who you can't forgive, those who annoy you, those who rub you the wrong way. You see, I placed those people in your life. They're not there by accident. I've placed them in your life so that both may grow, that you might grow more fully into my likeness and my image by sharing truth in love and gentleness, in mercy. If you love someone you would want to save them from danger, from darkness, from evil, would you not? Even for a stranger, if you saw them in danger and you saw they were going to walk across the street and a car was coming, you would do everything in your power to push them out of the way. You would do everything by speaking out to them and telling them "No, move back, step away, you're in danger!" But yet you fail to do it to the very people that you could help with a word, with the truth, spoken in love. Don't worry how they take it. Don't be concerned on what they think of you. Just love them in me, speak the truth because you care.

I thirst for souls and I place the power of my Spirit at work in you to accomplish the work that I send each of you out to do. There are some that I've brought into your life for a mission, a purpose, a strategic plan. I've blessed you through these people. I've spoken to your heart and you inclined your ear and so I say to you what you have received you must be able to speak. Speak it in the light. Speak it to those that you think might not accept it. Just speak it and allow me to water it so that their faith may grow, that in due season the light will dispel the darkness and sorrow would give way to joy, confusion to clarity, despair to hope. Be not afraid, do not fear. Trust me.

7/6/17 (1 of 2)

  I want to heal your weary souls. Many hearts are heavy. Many of you are weary. Many of you carry great burdens. But I call you to myself that I myself may give you rest, may give you the peace that you seek, the peace that I alone can give you.
  You will be in awe of the many things that are to come, but I tell you again, do not let your hearts be troubled or afraid. There will indeed be fires from the sky. The ground will tremble and there will be storms, but I tell you this: I say this to you that your heart and mind and spirit will be prepared. I will prepare you. You need only to remember to keep your eyes on me, to trust in the word that washes you, cleanses you, renews you, and strengthens you. Many a people have walked far away from me. Many have their own agenda. Many no longer listen to my word or receive the grace and sacramental life of the Church that I have left them and

because of this they will seek destruction, and in the end their own destruction.

    I am a God of power and might. I am a God of mercy and grace. There is no other god before me. I created heaven and earth. I am the Lord your God, there is no other. Every family on earth takes their name from me their heavenly Father. I will protect my own and so it is important when these things come to pass that you remember these words. This is in preparation for what will come to pass so that you might lead others back to the truth that will set them free. I ask you to trust in me, and more importantly, place your hope in me, for those who place their hope in me will never be put to shame. Again I tell you: Let not your heart worry or be afraid. I go before you and I prepare the way. Once again, many will fall on their knees, many will come back to me, many will come to know me for the first time, and it is you that will remember, it is you that will be at peace through the turmoil for I am calling my own. I place my protective seal over you, and I say again: This is an urgency, this is a time for you to be my missionaries, to be my living presence in the world which is in such desperate need. Come to me with your problems. Come to me when your heart is heavy. Do not seek your own wisdom but trust in wisdom from above.

7/6/17   (2 of 2)

I will awaken the whole Church to my power, to my love, and to my mercy. I will bring, once again, my mother to the forefront. All who seek refuge in her immaculate heart will always be carried into my own sacred heart. Safe you will be, not only you, but your whole household. Place your hope in me. Place your trust in me, and do not look what's happening afar off. Let not your hearts be troubled, let not your legs tremble, and let fear be far from you. Fear not for I am with you always. I will never leave you nor forsake you.

7/13/17

Many who know me and profess to love me hear my word, but they do not often listen to it. Many times they do not grasp what it is that I'm saying to them. They do not understand that when my word goes forth it goes forth to do a mighty work. When you are about a mighty work, the gates of hell will try to prevail against it, just like they will come against the Church, persecute the Church. Remember my words that the gates of hell will never prevail against my Church. You must remember that you are part of that Church. You must never forget that you are part of the mystical body and so I say to you: when you are about a mighty work, when you are walking to fulfill and act on my word, the gates of hell will try to come against you. Simply remember this: that you are mine. You are flesh of my flesh and bone of my bone. You are the mystical body ... my mystical body on earth ... and one day all will be one.

Even as I speak, many are being converted at this hour ... those that were thought to never believe in the Father and the Son and the Holy Spirit, thought never to believe and follow my one, holy, catholic and apostolic Church. This is the hour for conversions to take place. This is the time to be true to my word, to safeguard the doctrine, to be aware without any inner doubts that my word is true and that my word is protected by the power of my Holy Spirit and that my dogma will remain sound because I have entrusted it to those who I have called for a time such as this. I want you to know and never forget who you are: children of the most high God. Never forget that I have sent you to do the works that I have done and even far greater than those because I went to the Father and I left you my Spirit to carry on these works.

I want you to use the gifts that I have given to you. I want you to have eyes that see and ears that hear the truth, and the greatest truth that is often lost is this: *the word became flesh and dwells among you in every tabernacle all over the world.* This is the truth, and though many have left that truth going after and seeking a word that will tickle their ears, a word that will make them rich or famous, running after those that can not promise eternal life ... only I can do that. I am the resurrection and the life. But I am moving and pouring out my Spirit on all mankind. There is an urgency and in this time I would have you remember that I am the Lord your God who heals you. I am the Lord your God who breathed life into you ... the breath of God into you. You are my own and no one will snatch you out of my hand.

So though you be persecuted, though the gates of hell will try to come against you, be at peace. Remember, you don't belong to the world, you belong to me. Many will be called to sacrifice much, but I tell you this: it will not be in vane. In your time, this time, do not fear the enemy. You see, you do not have to do battle with the enemy. I will go before you and fight your battles, but you have to know, without an inner doubt, that I who am in you are far greater than he who is in the world. Even the "elite" will be fooled. Remain steadfast. Stay close to my eucharistic heart. Stay close to the sacramental life of the Church which will safeguard your heart, mind and spirit. Be at peace. Be at peace and know that my mother enfolds her mantle over you. Know that you are marked and sealed with the power of my Spirit. Every sacrifice you offer is not in vane. Every tear you shed I capture. It is never wasted.

For those who are wounded and hurting, broken, grieving, sick physically, mentally, spiritually or emotionally, remember my words: I am in you and working through you and I send you to do my work and I will work in you and through you. I only ask that you who have ears to hear, eyes to see, and a heart to receive stand in this truth. Never forget how important you are to me and how important it is to live your life in me with me and through me.

8/17/17

There's times you feel that I have forgotten you or have not heard the cry of your heart. I assure you, nothing could be further from the truth. You see, I hear every prayer. And do you know what really moves my heart? Do you know and understand that my heart rejoices when you surrender yourself into my hands? Of course you have your wants and your needs and your desires. I am your Lord and your God and I will meet every one of them, but many times, in ways that you can not see, feel, understand. Need I remind you that my ways are not your ways. But I rejoice when you surrender: "Not my will, but your will, Lord. Let your will be done in my life."

It was through the beautiful gifts of the saints in their lives that you can see, you can learn from, that even those that were burned at the stake my grace flooded through them, even those that laid down their life for another. For all generations that example is known to all. It is not always what you feel like doing, it is not always what you want to do in those times most difficult that you yield to my will not your will, and when you do I give you the desires of your heart often, and in the end, I always give you the desires of your heart when you seek my will, my way, my love.

I'm always blessing you and healing you, renewing you, even in the most difficult of times, the times of loss when you've lost someone that you love. I take you from grief to grace time and time again in times when you are suffering emotionally, physically, spiritually, mental anguish. In those times I am always working for your greater good. You do not see, you do not understand because my ways are not your ways. And so I bless you and give you grace, strength and courage to journey on through difficult times and circumstances then I bless and anoint and heal and renew and refresh and I bless you with a deep abiding joy that wells up within you when you say: "This is the Lord."

I want you to be a people of faith, of hope and trust knowing whatever you ask for I hear and many days through many years if you look back over your life you will praise and thank me for unanswered prayers because I always had a greater good for each of you in my heart, in my will. You see, I search the heart, mind and spirit and I see those that are worthy of receiving great gifts and I bless them mightily.

So I tell you to continue to move in me and allow me to work in you and through you for my greater glory so that my will will be accomplished. The kingdom of God is within you and I want you to know in those times, those sacrifices, those crosses, when you embrace the cross and you unite my will with your will, great things happen.

So be at peace in all circumstances. Praise me unceasingly at all times and your reward will be great and others who see you will definitely see me in you knowing surely it is the Lord. So again, my heart rejoices when you surrender your will to my will. Oh, I know it's a little bit at a time but the more you surrender and the more you grow in me the more at peace you will be in every situation. You are my own beloved. You are my beautiful beloved.

8/24/17

So many of my people, they grasp, they grasp at all that they can grab and all that they can take. They want it all ... money, popularity, fame, fortune, and they think that is where their hearts will be filled to overflowing happiness and joy. They forget my word to *seek first the kingdom of God and all other things shall be added unto them*, and so they continue to follow after their own desires. They continue to seek those things in their lives that they think will make them happy. Fools! Such fools they are because it's my life in exchange for their life that will fill them with a peace and a grace and a strength that others will see in them that will go beyond all understanding. It is that peace, that grace, that strength, that mercy, that love that others will be drawn to. Then one day they will realize that their lives are really empty but full of "things" and those "things" often times are their own destruction.

I prosper those who love me and serve me. I watch over my own. I want them to know without any doubt that I am, indeed, their Savior, their Redeemer, Son of the living God, that there is no other god beside me for I have made all things and nothing exists without me. I want my people to know and understand the depth of my love for them. I am not a God of rules and regulations. I am God, I am the one God, I am the Lord, the messiah, the Son of God who takes away all the sin of the world, and that so many refuse that love, so many walk away from that love, and the enemy comes and he sows in their midst seeds of ruin: pride, envy, hatred, jealousy, and this is why they seek after more, always more, because they do not realize that if they sought after me, the living God, the one triune God, that all other good things would come unto them. They do not understand that with me they have no need, and so I entrust to you this truth.

I want you to be able to make disciples. I want you to invite others. Tell them to come. Tell them to see for themselves that I alone am the very source and summit of all their peace, their love and their joy and their fulfillment. I will give you all that you need. I will bless you in your state in life to accomplish all that I call you to do. I did not promise you ever that there would be no trials or tribulation. I did not promise you that there would not be sorrow and pain and grief, but I did promise you that I would be with you always at every moment of every day. I did promise you that I have come to give you life and life to the full. I have come as your messiah, your Savior, your Redeemer. What more on earth is worth more to you than me? You can seek it all and find it, but is there anything worth, so much worth to you that you would be willing to give up your salvation.

Take this message out to the world. I alone am the way, the truth and the life. Go and make disciples. Invite them. It doesn't depend on you. Invite them and allow me to work in them and through them for there's nothing in this world, absolutely nothing, that is worth dying for and separating yourself from salvation. Take this message out.

9/7/17

My people, am I not the Lord your God ... the God of comfort, the God of peace, the God of mercy and love? I want to speak to your hearts now, in this moment, at this time. I do not want you to forget, I don't want you to ever forget that I am the God of love and mercy. I am the font of all mercy. I want to heal and bind up wounds. I want to wash away your burdens; I want to take them from you. Do you think that I don't know that in this time in your life you are concerned about what happens next? What is it Lord that you want from me in this time in my life? I know your concerns, I know your fears and your doubts and your anxiety, and so I say to you, I've brought you here to tell you: "Fear not. Let not your heart be troubled or afraid." I am at work in your lives in the ways that you see me and recognize me, but believe it or not, I am actively involved in <u>all</u> situations and circumstances even those that you can not see me, even those that you do not feel that I am present.

I know what it's like to be broken, to have a heart that is broken because you've been rejected, despised, not acknowledged. You feel that you often don't "make the mark." Often times you feel that you have failed, but I am here with you always. I want you to place your hope and your trust in my power ... my power to heal and to restore and to renew ... my power to reconcile ... my power to bring back those who are on the brink of going to hell, not because I send them there, but because they have closed their heart, their mind and their spirit and they choose to send themselves there. Never give up, my people. Never loose hope on one soul. Every soul I died for … I don't want one lost.

This is a time of great mercy. It's a time of urgency in the Church. There will be many tumultuous circumstances, many powerful storms in life that can totally devastate people. But yes, even in the midst of what seems to be hopeless, even in the midst of the lives when they feel that all is lost, when they feel there's no purpose for their life, that everything they have is gone, everything they seek to have they'll never accomplish … these are lies from the pits of hell. I tell you this: I am with you; I am working in your situations and circumstances, and one day you will look back and thank me. You will thank me because you have grown, because you allowed me to stretch you to find out that my God is always with me, my God is always present. If it wasn't for these situations and circumstances in your lives and the lives of your loved ones, in the lives of the people in authority, if it wasn't for those times you would surely be stifled. You would surely have lost faith and hope and trust. But it is a fact. It's an "absolute", it's not relative … I am with you and I am bringing you to a place in your life where you will experience peace where you thought you would experience upheaval and turmoil. I am bringing each of you to a place where you will be my hands and my feet and my voice.

Can I speak through you? Will you give me and offer me your voice? Will you offer me your heart that I might bind up wounds, wounds of the heart, mind and spirit, where your words have wounded or hurt someone? Will you allow me to work in you and through you to bring that healing balm, to bring that love and mercy and truth? Will you allow me to move in you and through you because in doing this you accomplish my will, something you seek to do in your mind and in your heart? But your will is weak and instead you go about with your desires, with your will, and that brings the cross into each of your lives. Instead of a straight line from you to me you place a cross because you want your will to be accomplished. You can not fix things that you have not broken. You can not heal what you have not wounded. You can not bring health and healing into minds, bodies and spirit ... only I can do that. My love and my light dispels the darkness. My light will always shine forth and brightly in the darkness to dispel it.

  I want you to be well grounded in the truth. I want you to forgive and I want you to be able to ask for forgiveness. I want you to be at peace so that I can use you to bring my peace into a world that will be enveloped in turmoil, devastation. I can not send you to bring peace, truth, mercy and life, new life ... you can not give what you do not have. And so I ask you, will you allow me to give you everything you need to be a light shining in the darkness, to be a voice crying out, "This is the way to go"? Will you allow me to use you to forgive and bind up wounds? You see, in forgiveness I have left you a word, my word: unless you forgive one another as I have forgiven you, you will not be forgiven. This is a sin against the Holy Spirit. You must forgive. It's not a feeling, my people. It's a decision and once you yield your will to my will the rest is easy. You see, I flood your soul with grace to forgive. I flood your soul with peace. I flood your soul with my light to dispel the darkness for as you forgive you will be forgiven.

And so I say to each of you who hear my word now, go out and be my mystical body. Go out into the deep. Do not stand in the shallow waters but enter the river of grace. Be soaked in the new living waters to bring hope where there is hopelessness, to bring light where there is darkness, to bring love where there's hate, to bring mercy where there's unforgiveness. These are true words and the truth will set you free.

9/14/17 (1 of 2)

You've heard the expression: "Hope springs eternal." I am hope itself, and all who place their hope in me will be renewed and strengthened. All those who place their hope in me will not be ashamed. I am eternal hope. I myself died that each of you might have life. I am the resurrection and the life. All else is temporary. Everything else will pass away. In these urgent times I ask you to remind yourself often to place your hope in me, not in your belongings, not in material goods, not in your businesses, not in people. I alone am your hope. I am the hope of the world. I alone will be their hope in the darkest hours, and so I ask you again to remember that I alone am the hope that the world must place their trust in, for those who do I will bless, protect and supply all their needs. I remind you that in hoping in me your strength will be full and renewed each day. I am the hope of the world that all would hear this truth and receive it before they are lost. I am the eternal light and the eternal life of this world. Place your hope in me and I will light your path even in the darkest of hours.

9/14/17 (2 of 2)

Let your ears be attuned to this truth ... I speak it clearly and concisely without being ambiguous in any way: There will be much to come to tickle your ears. These words will sound "right." They will seem to be full of sympathy and understanding. They will seem to be words of truth, but do not be deceived. These are words that the enemy brings to tickle your ears and the ears of those who do not have their heart, mind and soul set on me, and so it's easy to grab them with words that sound kind and good. Be attentive to this word.

Anything, anything at all that would contradict my Holy word, any teaching that would not be in accordance with what my one, holy, catholic and apostolic Church teaches is not truth. Truth will align with my Holy word. Truth will align with the dogma and the doctrine of my Church, the Church I founded. Truth will always align with the teaching magisterium. Do not be fooled with words that could tickle your ears, but stand in truth and do not be swayed. I do not contradict myself or teach contrary to what my Church teaches. I have protected and guided, through the Holy Spirit, the teachings of this one, holy, catholic and apostolic Church. It is universal. My desire is that all would come to be one in the fullness of truth. Do not compromise the teachings that have been handed down for you from Mother Church for they come from me. Again, the Holy Spirit has safeguarded these truths. Do not be deceived.

9/21/17

Each one of you are gifted. Each one of you have been blessed. You've been anointed by virtue of your baptism. I have given gifts to all. Like a beautiful symphony when each one plays their part, it is music that warms the heart and the soul. However, when you look at each other's gifts and seek after those, your gifts are lying dormant. I want you to realize that each one of you have a role to play so that you can all make a joyful noise unto the triune God ... Father ... Son ... Holy Spirit. We are one and you, though you are many, are all part of my one mystical body.

There is much evil springing forth more and more each day. I want you to remember that the darkness can never ever overcome the light. You fear. You get afraid. You doubt who I say I am. You forget the living word, my word that I left with each one of you showing you that I raised the dead, I gave sight to the blind, I healed all those who were brought to me that were under the influence of the Devil. I laid my hands upon the sick and they recovered. I called those forth out of darkness and they came by the authority of my word. Do you not realize even now that each one of you have a gift and I place you where I want you to be so that all of you together using your gifts will paint a beautiful tapestry through my hands, through my vision, through my work. For even in times when the Evil One comes against you, when all that you have is lost, when your pride or your dignity is wounded, when your heart is broken or crushed, when you feel there are no answers to your prayers, when you feel that I have closed my ears to the sound of your cry ... even then I am in the midst of each and every one of your lives.

I have talked about this darkness that pervades the earth right now and so many are so afraid of the darkness when really my light can dispel it. But you do not realize even now that you must take my light and allow it to shine through you working together for the good, working in the vineyard, so that I would bless all those that come to me through your work. Others come to me through someone's word. Others come through someone's witness. Others come through someone's music. Some come through the work of your hands. I could go on and on but I think you're beginning to understand that I want you to use your gifts. I'm pleased with you. My heart rejoices that you recognize that you are gifted. And I call you to share those gifts, and I bring you together to share those gifts, for the up-building of the body of Christ, and when all together use their gifts, it is a beautiful sound. It is music to my ears. It is a song in my heart.

Don't wonder and worry about the cost, what it will cost you. Believe me, I redeemed you "in full." I paid the price "in full" and all I ask is that you would allow me to work in you and through you to draw others to me. Do not be afraid of the dark. The dark can never dispel the light. Trust in me. Call to me and wait upon me and know that I will bless, anoint and lead, in you and through you, others into my kingdom.

9/28/17

Do you know what I'm thinking? I'm thinking that I look on you with love and I rejoice in who you are. I'm blessed that you are my disciples. I see all the ways that you struggle. I see times when you're very tentative. Even though you want to do certain things, you're intimidated, but I always give you another opportunity, don't I, until finally you step out and do what you've been called to do. I always know the struggle that goes on within when you seek to do my will and not your own. I know you don't blatantly choose your will over mine, but in the times that you do, I know afterwards you wish you would have done it my way instead of your way. But then I see that … I see the heart that's contrite. I see the heart that struggles to follow, and so I infuse you with grace again, and strength, strength for the journey, strength to step into the grace that I pour out for you day by day.

So you know what blesses my heart? You do, yes, you. When I see you hoping in me. When I see you trying to trust in me when you do not feel like trusting because you do not see how I am working in the situation and so it's difficult for you to trust. But I know that many times when you've placed your trust in others before, you have been wounded. Many times you've been betrayed. However, slowly but surely, I see you beginning to trust me, for each time that you do you see that I have worked everything together for good, not only for good but for a greater good. And so it is you that my heart rejoices over. You are mine, flesh of my flesh, bone of my bone. I look on you as a loving father and my heart rejoices when you accomplish things that you never thought you could do. But in me and with me and through me you see that all things are possible. You see that you can do all things in me who strengthens you.

I've seen you walk and stumble and fall, but you continue to get up again. You continue to walk in faith and go forward. You try to have ears to hear my word. Your desire seeks my will and I would tell you now, right now: do not get discouraged, do not beat yourself up, do not tear yourself down. That is a lie from the enemy so that you will loose heart, and when you fall he feels you will not get up again, but I know you better and I dispel the darkness that you feel, the disappointment, the discouragement, the depression, even the confusion and the doubt and then my light wells up within you dispelling those dark areas so that you can not only get up again but that you are strengthened in resolve through grace.

So I delight in my children. I delight as I watch you grow, as I watch you mature in the spirit. Just as you with earthly children hope only for the very best for your children, want only the best things for them, how proud of them you are when they accomplish their goals, how your heart rejoices when your children recognize me in their life. I am your father, you are my children, and I love each and every one of you and my heart rejoices with your "tries" and your "triumphs." Never doubt my love even though you feel me not, even though you hear me not, even though you see me not. Learn to recognize me in the ones I bring into your life who speak words of truth that will set you free. Recognize me in the one who reaches out to help you when others turn their back. Recognize me in the love that I shower upon you because I am in all those that I send into your life, the ones you recognize and the ones you're not even aware of. Trust me. I really do know what I'm doing.

10/5/17

I don't want you to worry about your children. Remember, they were mine before they were yours. I'm watching over them. I want you to realize that I knew them and loved them before you. I want you to entrust them into my care. I want you to place your worries and your anxieties and your cares on me. I want you to place them all at the foot of my cross. Did I not tell you that I took everything and nailed it to the cross with me? Did I not tell you that I am Lord over all and have control over all?

I'm not finished with you yet either. I'm full of surprises, full of new joys. I have a plan for each of you. I want you to realize that I am in every single instant, every single moment, every single hour, every single day. I am in the present moment and I am working in and through all those things that burden your heart, trouble your spirit. Can't you trust me? I make all things new. I bring new life into every situation, but I want you to surrender. I want you to surrender your children to me. I want you to surrender your life to me. I want you to surrender your business to me. I want you to surrender your ministry to me. I will not force myself upon you in those areas, but I tell you this: as you begin to surrender all those things, one by one slowly but surely, into my heart, I will fill you with a peace that you have not experienced since you first came into the Spirit. You see, when you empty yourself of the burdens that you carry, of the fears, the anxieties, for your children especially, for your friends, for your loved ones, and even for yourself, I want you to realize that it's then that you will be free and open to experience a new infilling of my Holy Spirit. I want to empower you. I want to heal you. I want to renew you in mind and body and spirit. I have so much more that I want to give you. I'm a "God of more", you know ... more love, more mercy, more peace, more strength, more grace for the journey. And so I ask that you begin to ponder this truth that the more you give to me and empty yourself that I will fill you with living water, with new life, with the fire of my Spirit. I will burn away all those things that will stifle the Spirit of God at work in you.

  I will enter into your children's lives when you step back. I will give you the peace to watch when you allow me to work freely in them and through them. I was patient with you, wasn't I? Be patient with them and know I did not leave you alone, I did not forsake you even in the most difficult of times, so know that I will not forsake them even in the most difficult of times. You see, my ways are not your ways … remember that. But I am working in and through all things. When you see things as hopeless, when you see things getting worse, when you see things that don't seem to have any sense of awe of my being present in the situation, know for sure that though you see me not or feel me not, I am truly present.

So come on … open your heart … all those things that trouble you, hand them to me, offer them to me so that I might place in their place: peace, grace, strength, courage, hope and so much more.

10/12/17

I see the joy that's in your heart tonight. I see the lightness in your step. I see the lightness in your heart. You did not know that I had a surprise for you. You thought you were going in one direction and I turned you around to go in another direction … gently, very gently I turned you. But because you love me with all your heart, confused and doubting many times, you trusted, and because you trusted you have seen my plan being revealed to you slowly but surely. Did I not tell you that I would give you a surprise of the Spirit? Was not my word spoken to you? A surprise of the Spirit indeed. For each of you I say, eye has not seen nor ear has not heard of the surprises that I still have in store for you.

With you I am pleased. You died to yourself and in obedience followed what you knew was my call on your life. You sought my will over yours and you were sorrowful, even unto grief, but I began to put a new song back in your heart. You always knew that I had a plan. Did I not call you myself? Did I not send you? Did I not bring you to the place where you have found growth, gifts ... gifts that you didn't even know you had? Yes, I am the God of surprises.

But you must remember that the enemy would sow you with doubt, would fill you with misgivings, would try to bring division, but I tell you this: my heart rejoices that you trusted me, that you were sorrowful, that you repented, and that you were filled with a new peace. You see, you can always tell when the enemy is at hand. He might fill you with the things of the world. He might give you feelings that you think are good, but he can not give you peace ... not ever, and so when your spirit is in unrest, when you don't seem to have peace, when you seem like you really don't even know which way to go ... that's the enemy because even when you're not sure of which way to go, when you're following me, I put a peace within your spirit. You've learned a great truth: the enemy can never give peace. He is not one of love or mercy or compassion. He imitates the gifts so that you will be tripped up, that you would be perplexed, confused, angry, resentful. He's only a cheap imitation.

But you, you have experienced the love and mercy and power of the true and only living God. I have more to come ... more surprises. I want to bring my joy to completeness in you. I want to expand your joy. I want to fill you with peace where there is unrest because I am a God of surprises. I will bring new surprises into your life this week and you will say: "This is the Lord." You will remember my words and they will well up within you and your heart will be rejoicing and grateful that you have waited and stood in faith, in hope, in trust, in belief of my power at work in every situation.

10/19/17

Do you realize that each of you are mine ... that I'm in love with each of you ... that you were created in my own likeness and image, in Our likeness and image you were created. And so I want to remind you, never forget, not for a moment, how much you're loved. Never forget that you are children of the most high God, too. Never forget that you're so loved, so deeply loved, that I went to the cross for you that you might be with me forever in paradise. You do belong to me. I paid the price fully and completely ... paid up in full. There is nothing you could ever do to earn my love or the gift of your salvation. It has been done. It is finished.

And so as you walk throughout this journey I would have you remember that you are a living witness, that I am living in you and moving through you. In the darkest of times I want your light to shine brightly. I want to dispel your anxieties and your fears and your worries. I know many have heavy hearts, many of you have had broken dreams, many of you have trials to suffer ... physical trials, spiritual trials, emotional trials, and in those times I ask you to remember who you belong to. I want you to remember that I will never leave you nor forsake you. I want you to remember that each one of you have been redeemed by my blood and interiorly I have placed my love, my power, my anointing and my joy in your heart ... a joy that can overcome any sadness... a peace that will go beyond all understanding. That's what I have given you: my joy that your joy could be complete; my power to help you live out your faith, for it is my power at work in you that gives you the strength and the grace to be a witness. On your own it can not be accomplished but it is my power at work in you, my love which I have consecrated you in. You are my joy. You are my delight.

In the times that are coming I would never have you doubt that I am still Lord and in control over everything. All belongs to me. The heavens and the earth, I created all. All life I created. Each of you, each and every one of you were in my mind before you were ever in your mother's womb. And so know that I will never leave you and in the darkest of times trust in my love. I will lead you and guide you and direct you. Do not be afraid. Do not fear. Do not loose hope for I alone am hope itself. I have a plan. My plan will be carried out. Trust in me and not in what you see or hear. Trust in my love and in my word that I am with you always, that I am in the midst of even the darkest of times to bring the light to dispel them.

My mother's heart will be victorious ... the Immaculate ... my masterpiece ... my mother ... my spouse. Know this: she is interceding before my Father. She is interceding for more time, more grace. I tell you this: I have so much in store for you to bless you, to set you free completely, to renew you in mind and body and spirit. No matter what you hear, no matter what you see, know that I am Lord over all and that there is nothing you need fear, for with me you have no needs.

10/26/17

Sometimes you feel you're so busy. You're rushing from the time you get up till the time you go to bed in the evening. Little do you know that you feel this pressure to rush, you feel that you're not going to get things accomplished that you had planned to do and so you leave me out of your day because you don't have time to pray. But I tell you, when you take the time to pray you'll have time left over at the end of your day because I will be Lord over your entire day, and remember, I work all things together for good.

I don't think you realize, I'm speaking to each of you right now at this moment, I don't think you realize the efficaciousness of prayer. I don't think you realize the power in righteous people who pray. If you did you would pray all the more. You would pray all the more fervently as well, because when you pray you're entrusting everything into my hands. When you pray you're placing everything under my control. Do you doubt that my ways are not your ways but indeed they will be the most perfect ways?

Too busy are you? Too busy for me? You don't have time you say. Foolish people. Every moment, every instant you have is because I have given you breath. I have given you *"Ruah"*, the breath of my Spirit. You see, I'm outside of time and space. I am not under any constraint. I have no limits on me for I am the Creator of heaven and earth and so I remind you that when you pray know that I will go before you; know that I hear the cry of your heart; know that I am working in every single situation and then you will not be anxious, you will not be afraid, you will realize that you must trust in me and not in yourself. So many times you rely on yourself rather than to depend on me and that's why so often you can not understand why things don't work out the way you want them to and you blame it on me. You blame it on me cause it's easier than looking deep within and realizing that in many ways through many days it's things that you yourself are doing or not doing that often stifle the power of my Spirit at work for you go your way instead of my way. You carry out your plan instead of my plan. You don't even stop to ask me. You just move ahead.

And so I say, slow down. Take time to pray. Take time to be still and know that I am God. Take time to realize that I love you more than you could ever possibly imagine. When that truth touches your heart, when it sinks deep into your heart, your trust will expand and your anxiety and your fears and your concerns will dissipate. So slow down a bit. Begin your day with me and invite me to go throughout the day with you and you will see so many surprises in your day that I have brought about. Rather than just rushing through the day and missing all those little expressions of my love, rushing through the day and not even seeing or experiencing those little moments I put of joy, excitement, healing, friendship, relationships ... I put so much in your day, but because you rush through it you do not take the time to see them, to experience them and so at the end of the day you ask: "Where are you?" My answer will always be: "With you. Are you with me?"

11/02/17

I want you to learn from me for as it is written: "I am meek and humble of heart." Do not think that to be "humble" means to not think much of yourself or in any way to think that you're not worth much, you're not gifted, you're not talented, or nothing goes right for you. Don't think that that means "humility." Nothing could be further from the truth. You see, humility is when you take your eyes off of yourself ... when you want to serve; when you want to be my hands, my feet, my voice; when you bring my heart to those who have lost hope; when you bring the fire of my love to those who are lost and the brightness of that fire leads them back to me. When you worry about yourself that you're not good enough, smart enough, wealthy enough, attractive enough, popular enough ... do you see what I mean ... your eyes are on yourselves.

But when you look to others and recognize that you have the greatest gift within you. ... the gift of my

Holy Spirit abiding in you, then it's always about bringing me to others, focusing on other's needs, lending a helping hand to others, giving comfort and consolation to those who are hurting, broken or wounded or have no hope. True humility points away from one's self, points to others, points to me for my glory and honor. You see, that's how it is with the Trinity and the fullness of Father, Son and Holy Spirit. Didn't the Father point to me the entire time … always pointed to His Son, promised His Son, pointed to His Son? And did I not point to the power, to the love between my Father and me in the person of my Holy Spirit? Did I not point to Him and give honor and glory to my Spirit?

So I just want to remind you, true humility is not about tearing yourself down or thinking less of yourself, quite the contrary. True humility is praising God for all the ways He has blessed you and given you gifts, for all the things that He's given you and all the things that He's taken. It's about giving glory and honor to your Triune God. It's about being my hands, my feet, my voice, my heart to others.

11/30/17 (1 of 2)

Are you uncomfortable with the quiet? Do you feel like you need to say something or sing something or do something? I tell you truly that I do speak the loudest in the silence of your hearts. I call you to come away with me to a quiet place to prepare your heart, prepare your heart day in and day out for my coming. I come each day anew you know, each and every day. I visit you and sometimes you recognize my visitations. You are amazed and you say: "This must be the Lord." But you see, I come and rest within you, speak quietly to you. Many times I watch over you while you're sleeping just like you did with your children ... and I love you. I look at you lying there in the night and my heart swells for love of you. If only you would recognize me throughout the day more often.

You see, I alone can calm your fears. I can calm the storm in your lives. I can turn your sorrow into a joy, a joy that will run deep within your heart, your soul, your mind and your spirit, even in the midst of great sorrow, because it's my joy that is complete in you when you put your hope and trust in me. I have seen your struggles, your fears. Oh, I know all about your anxiety. I know about your broken relationships. I know about all the things that you worry about and I want to heal your heart. I want to bring my light deep within the deepest recesses of your soul to dispel the darkness that's there ... the resentment, the fear, the guilt, and yes, even shame. You see, I came that you might have life in abundance and that's why I visit you. I visit you and I move within your spirit and I prompt you all throughout the day and maybe once in a day you'll recognize it is the Lord. But if you'd be still, if you open your heart and your eyes and your ears you would see that I'm with you all the time. I never ever leave you. I have given you many gifts but you're so caught up in the past you can't live fully in the present. Your mind is back on what you should have done, could have done, wish you would have done, but you see, I'm always in the present moment. I am the "Now."

Will you give me permission to be Lord over your life? Will you begin, day by day, moment to moment, to surrender all the things that fill your heart with resentment or bitterness, unforgiveness, jealousy, yes, even hatred. You see, I will make all things new. So trust me. Trust me to love you into wholeness in the midst of your brokenness. When you call to me I will come to you and I will speak loudly in the silence of your heart.

11/30/17   (2 of 2)

I also tell you that you have not been to confession. You see, this sacrament is healing, it's my healing balm and as you confess and go to the sacrament of confession I will give you a new heart. I will remove the darkness and fill you with light. I would take away your sorrow, your shame, your guilt, your resentment and your bitterness, and I will give you new life. This is what I call you to my child ... new life. I have more that I want to give you but if I told you now you wouldn't be able to consume it all. You wouldn't be able to fully grasp it.

Come away to a quiet place indeed, you and I in the sacrament of the present moment. And in the sacrament of confession I will reconcile you with others. I will renew you and I will give you back the joy of your salvation and I will create in you a clean heart and you will come to bless my holy name. You are my child and I will never leave or forget you.

12/14/17 (1 of 2)

I want to transform you and I want to mold you more perfectly into my likeness and image. I want to shine my light into the darkness in those areas that you hide from everyone but me, because I know all and see all. But I tell you I am the Divine Physician ... I am the one ... I AM ... there is no other. I tell you today, this very day, this very evening, that I am pouring out my Spirit anew. I am shining my light into the deepest recesses of your heart. I see the pain, the helplessness, the suffering. I see all the gifts that I have given you. Many of these gifts are just lying dormant within you. But I want to guide you. I want to lead you. But first I must prepare your heart, your mind and your spirit so that when others see you, when others hear you, they will know, indeed, that it is me moving in you, loving in you, being merciful through you, reaching out with a healing word, calming a spirit, bringing peace where there's turmoil. Allow me to be Lord over every area of your life. Do not trust in anything, any spirit ... all else are deceivers. I alone AM. I alone am the way and the truth and the life, there is no other. I have come to set you free. I have indeed come to mold you and transform you, not to be someone else, but I love you just the way you are, and so I want you to be all that you are called to be, all that you were created to be, my child. I want to refresh you because you have lost the joy of your salvation. You've grown weak and weary of the journey and I want to refresh you and renew you. I want to put zeal in your heart. I want enthusiasm to well up within you and flow out to others so they too will come and see, so they too will come and follow me.

For every hurt, every wound, every doubt, every fear, I will give you the remedy. The remedy is "truth." The truth alone can set you free. I will give you my light to dispel the darkness. And I, myself, will mold and fashion you more perfectly into my likeness and my image. You see, I want to use you. I want you to come willingly to the font of all mercy and love because I have a plan for you … a plan to bless you, to prosper you, a plan to speak in you and through you.

Will you surrender to me? Will you invite me into your heart and allow me to be Lord over your decisions? For I will make straight your path so that you might go out and be one of my wounded healers reaching out in love and mercy in compassion, and reaching out with the power of my Holy Spirit, because apart from my Spirit, living and moving and dwelling in you, you will not be able to bear fruit that will last. I am the God of the impossible. I have come to make things new. Much will pass away but my word will never pass away.

So come a little closer. Invite me into your heart because I do have a plan for you. I have a plan to give you eyes to see things you never saw before, ears to hear my word and my voice deep within the recesses of your heart and soul. Yes, you! Will you allow me? Will you invite me to come into your heart, your mind, your will, your imagination and allow me to be Lord over it all? When you can, I will not force myself upon you, and when you can say "Here I am", when you can say "Come into my heart, Lord, I need you. Come Lord Jesus." When you are able to say "Jesus is Lord", then I will fill you with a power and a grace and a strength that goes beyond all understanding. These are gifts, my gifts to you.

    I wait. I wait for you to invite me to be Lord of your life and to allow me to work in you and through you to be a light in the darkness.

12/14/17 (2 of 2)

    You will know tomorrow. As you leave here and you sleep this night, I will speak and whisper quietly to you. You will know without a doubt that I have called you. You will know without a doubt that it is time for a new beginning. You will know without a doubt that I am loving you into wholeness. You will know without a doubt that we have come together in the Spirit of my love. You are mine and I am yours. All you need is to ask, to invite me in, and I will come.

(END OF VOLUME X)